A NEW KIND OF JOY

A
New Kind of Joy

THE STORY OF
THE SPECIAL OLYMPICS

by James Haskins

DOUBLEDAY & COMPANY, INC., GARDEN CITY, NEW YORK, 1976

Photo credits

The Joseph P. Kennedy, Jr., Foundation: 1 (by Joe Gall); 8; 12; 13 (by Neil Nordlinger); 14 (by Neil Nordlinger); 15 (by Gerry Vuchetich); 16; 18; 19; 20. United States Army: 5 (by Pvt. Mike Moore); 21 (by PFC William E. Harper). Kansas Special Olympics Committee: 2; 3. Angela Myers, Mankato, Minnesota *Free Press*: 4; 11; 17. Carol Politis: 6; 23. Thomas Bowersock, editor, *Special Olympics: What It Means to Me* (Indiana State University, Terre Haute) 1974: 7; 28. Boca Raton, Florida *News*: 22. Bill Kneen: 24. Central Michigan University Information Service: 25; 29. Indiana Special Olympics Committee: 9; 26. Montana Special Olympics Committee: 27. Helen Brush Photography: 30. ISU-AVC Photo: 10.

Library of Congress Cataloging in Publication Data

Haskins, James, 1941-
   A new kind of joy.

   1. Physical education for mentally handicapped children. I. Title.
GV445.H37   790.19′6
ISBN: 0-385-03902-6
Library of Congress Catalog Card Number 75-14825

FOREWORD

The roll of drums and the blare of horns pierce the summer afternoon air, and the field is a mass of color and activity. At a commanding location on a crowded, bunting-draped platform, celebrities—politicians, sports personalities, film and television stars—stand in review as phalanxes of marchers behind bold identifying banners pass by while spectators cheer them on. At first glance, it is just another summer athletic festival, but upon closer inspection, it is not. It is a particularly special occasion, for the marchers are mentally retarded.

Somehow, though, they do not look quite the way "normal" people think that retarded people look. They stand straighter and their movements are more co-ordinated;

they march purposefully. Their expressions range from utter seriousness to wide grins, but there is pride in the eyes of all. They have come to compete in Special Olympics Games. It is indeed a special day for these people who, traditionally, have not had the opportunity to participate in very much that is special in the usual sense of the word. Traditionally, it is they who have been the spectators, watching the world march by. . . .

Nowhere has lack of opportunity for the retarded been more evident than in the area of sports and physical activity. For the non-retarded, sports are an integral part of life itself. Neighborhood playgrounds are scenes of continual activity from dawn to dusk, and one can mark the change of seasons as accurately there as on a calendar. In summer, makeshift diamonds are prepared for the summer game. As fall approaches footballs come out of garages and closets. In colder climates, winter means hockey and ice skating, and in the spring playground hoops are repaired for basketball. In school, physical education is part of the curriculum. Sports teams abound, whether school- or community-sponsored. What town does not have its Little League? But all these activities have traditionally been reserved for normal children—not for the mentally retarded. Sports were considered too dangerous for the retarded, too difficult for them to master, *wasted* on the retarded. Rarely did normal society realize the retarded had never been given a chance to prove otherwise.

"The mentally retarded may not be able to do everything normal children can, but they have a right to try," says Eunice Kennedy Shriver. "They know what they are missing. They know especially when they are missing the fun of play—of competition—of success."

The purpose of Special Olympics is to give all the retarded the opportunities they have missed.

ACKNOWLEDGMENTS

Of course, this book would not have been possible without the co-operation and help of the Joseph P. Kennedy, Jr., Foundation and Special Olympics, Inc., and I would like to thank, specifically, Mrs. Eunice Kennedy Shriver, Mrs. Beverly Campbell, Ms. Jane Gardner, Mr. Herb Kramer, and General Robert Montague. Thanks also to my editor, Mr. Stewart Richardson, who believed in this project.

I am grateful as well to the many people who consented to be interviewed for this book and/or who were so hospitable to me during my visits to various State Special Olympics Games:

In Indiana, former state directors Ms. Judy Campbell

and Dr. Thomas Songster; also, Ms. Mary Ann Pierce and Ms. Susan McCammon, Mr. and Mrs. Charles Gorrell and Jerry Joe Gorrell.

In Maryland, Mr. Thomas Carski, state director, and Ms. Mollie Picciotto, executive secretary, Sister Kevin Toy and Mr. Curt Conley, Mr. and Mrs. Robert Wiedel and Karl Wiedel.

In Washington, Mr. Ernest Hoff, former state director, Mr. Dave Anderson, Washington Special Olympics co-ordinator, Mr. and Mrs. Lawrence West and Julie West, Mrs. Catherine Conn and Steve and Susan Conn, and Lieutenant Colonel Paul Mernaugh, formerly of Fort Lewis Army Base, now of Picatinny Arsenal, Dover, New Jersey.

I am also grateful to Ms. Pat Condon, state director, Illinois Special Olympics, Mr. James E. Griffith, managing editor, Bakersfield *Californian*, Mr. Rafer Johnson, head coach of the National Special Olympics, Mr. M. LeRoy Reynolds, state director, Michigan Special Olympics and 1975 international games director, and Mr. Gary O. Totland, state director, Utah Special Olympics.

Thanks also to Mr. Milt Allen of Terre Haute, Indiana, Mr. Manni Kajjaria of Mt. Pleasant, Michigan, and Ms. Carol Politis of New York City for their fine photographic work. Mr. Thomas Bowersock, Lieutenant Colonel Coor of Fort Lewis Army Base, Boca Raton, Florida, *News*, Fort Lauderdale, Florida, *News*, and Mankato, Minnesota, *Free Press* were sources of photographs and other illustrative material for consideration, as were the following State Special Olympics Committees: Alabama, Connecticut, Indiana, Kansas, Michigan, Montana, New

Jersey, North Dakota, Texas, Vermont, and Washington.

Mrs. Mary Ellen Arrington typed the manuscript drafts, and I am grateful to her. A very special thanks to Kathy Benson, who helped to pull it all together.

CONTENTS

INTRODUCTION

We Americans love sports so much that we have made great athletes our most popular heroes. Their exploits earn headlines. We cheer their skill and grace. We try to be like them in strength and courage.

This is a book about some very special athletes who may set no records and make no headlines. But Jerry Joe Gorrell, Susan Conn, Karl Wiedel, Julie West, Mike Baker, and the hundreds of thousands of champions they represent are heroes well worth our knowing and deserving of our cheers.

They are mentally retarded. For years they had almost no chance at all to become athletes. Our sports-minded society even denied them the chance to play. We kept them out of public gymnasiums, swimming pools, and playgrounds. We shut them in institutions where their bodies as well as their minds became rusty with disuse.

Then came Special Olympics, a program of physical fitness and sports competition exclusively for the retarded. Suddenly, we began to recognize that millions of Americans who were condemned as "different" are very much like the rest of us. They love to play. They have great courage and perseverance. They have a capacity for joy and sharing which lifts the spirit and reminds us what sports is really all about.

In this book, you will meet many of these wonderful people, their families, the volunteers who have helped them so much. I am happy that Jim Haskins has told their stories so sensitively and in such detail. The Special Olympics Games have been well reported in newspapers and on television. But seldom has a skilled writer recorded in any depth the struggles and victories which take place even before the starting line is reached.

This book should do much to change our perspective of the unique individuals who have been fated to wear the label, "mentally retarded." It should make us aware of how unfairly we have treated them. We should come away with a new respect for them as persons; a new appreciation of what they can contribute to their families, their communities, and the nation.

By any standards of personhood, the mentally retarded measure up to our highest perceptions of what a human being should be. When we take the time to teach them, they show courage and skill. When we show them respect and friendship, they are loyal and devoted friends in return. When we give them their just rights, they are good and productive citizens.

Today, millions of the mentally retarded are in school or on the job. In the federal government alone, more than twelve thousand are performing important and useful tasks. Many others have proven to have marketable skills in arts and crafts.

For many of the participants, Special Olympics has been their first experience of success; the first time they have heard anyone say, "Well done"; the first time they have recognized in themselves the ability to meet a difficult challenge.

To put it most simply, through Special Olympics, the mentally retarded are becoming healthy. We know that regular exercise will produce better co-ordination, muscle tone, strength, and speed. Special Olympians are developing these physical qualities through their year-round training programs. But, beyond this, they are experiencing health in other significant dimensions.

Because of new skills and accomplishments, they have a healthier regard for themselves. Because their parents, brothers, and sisters see them achieving results, they are developing healthier family relationships. Because friends and neighbors are able to share in their sports activities, there is a healthier acceptance on the part of the community. Through Special Olympics, many of the mentally retarded are coming home to enjoy the rights of full citizenship.

But Special Olympics reaches only about 20 per cent of those who can benefit from it. For every young athlete

Jim Haskins describes, there are four more standing on the sidelines waiting to take part.

I hope Jim's book will prove not only a stirring tribute to the Olympians who are, but a reminder of all those Olympians still to become. No reader should put this book down satisfied that the job has been done. For there are 2.5 million children and young adults in America and millions more elsewhere in the world who have no caring friend like Special Olympics.

In every state and many foreign countries, there are Special Olympics chapters which need volunteer health and support. If this book touches your heart and stirs your conscience, get in touch with your local Special Olympics chapter or write to me. Somewhere in your community there is a Special Olympian waiting to be discovered; a citizen waiting to be taught; a good friend waiting for the friend you can be.

It is in the thousands of acts of friendship which Special Olympics represents that we begin to create a truly human society, a society where, as President John F. Kennedy said, "the strong are just and the weak secure."

Eunice Kennedy Shriver
November, 1975

A NEW KIND OF JOY

Chapter I: The Special Olympics: How They Began, Where They Are Today

Colonel Red Blaik, coach of so many great Army football teams, devised a play featuring the "lonesome end." When the teams huddled, the lonesome end stood near the sidelines. As the teams lined up he remained isolated and almost unnoticed—far from the rest of the formation. When the ball was snapped he would quickly move downfield and be ready for a pass, frequently catching the opposition by surprise.

The mentally retarded are the lonesome ends of our society. At home, in school, in the community, they are always near the sidelines. Watching the action. Never allowed in the huddle.

Sadly the ball is never thrown to them, even though, with great willingness, they are ready to do their best. Simply because society regards them as different, the mentally retarded have traditionally been kept out of the game. —Eunice Kennedy Shriver

Our society has always feared what it does not understand, and has tried to isolate it, to shut it away from view. While other societies have recognized the "specialness" of the mentally retarded, for example, and revered them, historically we have dealt with the retarded by placing them in asylums or labeling them "village idiots." While our attitude toward, and treatment of, the retarded have become significantly more enlightened in this century, the majority of non-retarded people still suffer from massive ignorance of retardation. It is not enough that the terms "special children" or "special education" enjoy fairly wide use in America. Too many Americans continue to shrink from the retarded, to overprotect them or overpity them or use a variety of other defenses to keep from dealing with them as fellow human beings.

There is no racism in the world of retardation. There is no hatred. In their place, there is love and trust. "Normal" society could learn much from its retarded citizens. Instead, people of so-called higher intelligence tend to be put off by, and to isolate, the retarded under the guise of protecting them. Thus isolated, the opportunity of the retarded to show their capabilities is effectively rendered nil. They are indeed the "lonesome ends" of our society.

Persons who are incomplete by the standards of society have traditionally been provided incomplete opportunities to live and grow and develop their capabilities. This has been particularly true in the areas of athletic training and physical activity. While they have been kept out of the general game of life, they have been kept specifically out of the games that the non-retarded, especially non-retarded children, are encouraged to play. It is a traditionally held concept that the mind and body grow and develop together, and that a balance must be maintained in order for a child to grow up physically and mentally healthy. Any attack on the necessity for physical education and training for young people of normal intelligence has been consistently and vigorously opposed.

Not so for mentally retarded children. Physical activity was considered by many as unnecessary for the mentally retarded as for terminally ill patients. The attitude was that mental and physical development went hand in hand. Sport required the constant interaction of mind and body. The retarded could not be expected to develop mentally; therefore, it was useless to invest personnel and money in the physical development of the retarded. The result of this attitude was, of course, that the lack of opportunity to engage in physical activity often caused the mentally retarded to become physically retarded as well—and, sadly, even more retarded mentally.

While the importance of physical activity had always been taken for granted by most Americans, it was not until John F. Kennedy became President that there developed a national stress upon it. President Kennedy established a President's Council for Physical Fitness and Sports and emphasized the need for physical exercise, and his emphasis led to a renewed interest in the importance of physical activity for Americans. Researchers and research institutes began to conduct studies on the physical activity of Americans. Fortunately, some of these studies focused on the mentally retarded, and the results they showed led to further in-depth research.

By 1967, extensive research had been done in the area of physical activity and the mentally retarded, and this research had clearly established that the primary reason for lack of physical proficiency among the retarded was lack of opportunity for physical activity. Incredibly, approximately 45 per cent of all retarded children received no physical education at all, and only about 25 per cent received as much as an hour per week. Studies in Canada had shown that the physical performance of trainable retarded children (IQs 20 to 50) averaged four to six years behind normal children. They had half the strength of normal children of the same age, tired 30 per cent faster and carried 35 per cent more fat. Other research had established that many retarded children could equal or even surpass the performance levels of some normal children if given a chance to develop their skills. One pilot project showed that in just six months, trainable retarded children doubled their strength and endurance through regular physical activity.

The Kennedy family reacted in a major way to the results of these studies, although the family had been aware of, and concerned with, the need for physical activity for the mentally retarded long before the results of the studies were publicized. Physical fitness is part of the family code, and nowhere in America are athletics stressed more than in Kennedy households. Also, the Kennedys know personally about mental retardation, for one of the daughters of Joseph and Rose Kennedy was born re-tarded. They know firsthand how important physical activity is for a mentally retarded person.

The importance of such activity for the retarded is not only physical, but mental and emotional as well. The mental and physical demands of sport require constant co-ordination. Muscles are able to develop and strengthen according to natural and necessary movements. The mind is able to grasp concepts such as discipline, following in-structions, awareness of distance, understanding of time concepts. Mind and body begin to work together in tim-ing, balance, speed, to the benefit of both.

Sports are also important for the emotional and psycho-logical development of the retarded. Adjustment to sur-roundings includes awareness of other players and the learning of attitudes of sportsmanship. Team sports, espe-cially, require learning how to co-operate with others.

One of the most important effects of sports for the retarded, as for the non-retarded, is the feeling of accom-plishment. Human beings need to feel important and suc-cessful in at least one or two major areas of living. The mentally retarded face constant experiences of failure and frustration. Sports give them the opportunity to contrib-ute and to feel a part of something in which every-one engages. It gives them the chance to feel "special," a feeling all of us need.

As far back as 1963, the Joseph P. Kennedy, Jr., Foun-dation, in co-operation with the American Alliance for Health, Physical Education and Recreation, developed a physical fitness program for the mentally retarded and offered awards for achievement. It was a first step toward encouraging programs of physical activity for the retarded, but further steps could not be taken at that time, for the need for such programs was not recognized by the general public. By 1967, the increased number of studies involving physical fitness and the mentally retarded, and wider publication of the results of those studies, had caused the public to be more receptive to the idea that the mentally retarded needed and deserved programs of physical training. Almost spontaneously, it seemed, some individuals and groups across the country began to be interested in responding to those needs.

In Chicago, the Chicago Park District was considering a track meet for the retarded and, aware of the interest of the Kennedy family in such programs, inquired of the Foundation as to the national potential of the meet. The Foundation was interested. In the next two months the proposed track meet and its possibilities were discussed, and after careful consideration the Foundation decided to support the Chicago proposal. It was decided that the event would include not only track events but swimming events as well and that it would be an "Olympics" for the retarded, patterned somewhat after the Greek Olympics. Such an event would attract national interest and would enable the public to see the retarded in situations where they could participate and enjoy sports and show their capabilities. If the meet was successful, it could be the basis for a nationwide program of athletic training for the retarded.

Letters were sent out to every state in the Union. Would the state be interested in sending some of its retarded citizens to participate in a Special Olympics in Chicago? Reaction to the invitation was mixed. Many states reported that there just was not enough support for sports for the retarded. Any traditionally held attitude is slow to die, and the feeling that physical activity programs were wasted on the mentally retarded was particularly strong. "What good will it do?" was a common reaction, at first.

There were other reactions. Won't the meet be too much for the participants? Won't they become too excited? Will they be able to take the competition? Won't those who go to Chicago become fearful in the strange surroundings? Who will take the responsibility of transporting a retarded child or adult far away from home and familiar surroundings to be subjected to this stressful situation? How will they react to failure if they lose? When they must fail in so many other areas, how can they stand to fail in athletic competition as well?

Despite such misgivings, a substantial number of states responded affirmatively to the idea of the Special Olympics, and Canada, too, wanted to participate. The Chicago event would be an "International" Special Olympics. Encouraged by this evidence that Special Olympics was an idea whose time had come, the Kennedy Foundation approved a $20,000 grant for the International Special Olympics, and, at a press conference in Chicago in March, Mrs. Eunice Kennedy Shriver and Chicago Mayor Richard Daley officially announced the event, which would be held in July at Soldier Field.

During the next four months, Kennedy Foundation and Chicago Park District personnel worked busily organizing the events, establishing age and performance criteria for participation, and attending to the other myriad details involved in the ambitious undertaking.

Meanwhile, organizations, teachers, and even parents of the retarded in various states were selecting and training them for participation, raising funds, arranging for chaperons, getting the necessary medical releases and parental consent forms signed, and preparing the participants for the most exciting experience they had ever had.

On July 20, 1968, one thousand youths aged eight to seventeen from twenty-four states, Washington, D.C., and Canada began that experience with the opening ceremonies of the International Special Olympics in Chicago. The Great Lakes Naval Training Center Band led the participants, carrying state and school flags, in a parade of the states past the reviewing stand where they were welcomed by Mrs. Shriver and Mayor Daley and a number of other celebrities and dignitaries. A seventeen-year-old retarded youth carried the Special Olympics torch into the stadium and ignited the forty-foot-high John F. Kennedy Flame of Hope. The Special Olympics flag was raised, and two thousand helium balloons were released into the sky.

Over two hundred separate competitions took place in such events as the standing broad jump, 300-yard run, softball throw, 25-yard swim, 100-yard swim, high jump, and the 50-yard dash. Immediately after each event, gold, silver, and bronze medals were awarded to the first-, second-, and third-place winners. Each entrant also received a Special Olympics patch to signify his participation. When they were not competing, the participants had the opportunity to learn skills in various clinics taught by professional athletes who had been asked by the Foundation to help.

The athletic events and clinics spanned a two-day period. When the participants were not at Soldier Field they were at the "Special Olympic Village," into which the LaSalle Hotel, owned by the late U. S. Olympic Committee chairman, Avery Brundage, had been transformed for the weekend. There, all one thousand participants, coaches, and chaperons were housed in a dormitorylike atmosphere, ate their meals, and enjoyed evening entertainment together.

At the closing ceremonies at Soldier Field the participants, proudly wearing their patches and medallions and medals, locked arms with the coaches, chaperons, officials, and dignitaries and sang "Auld Lang Syne" as the Special Olympics torch was carried from the stadium and the flags were lowered. It was a perfect end to their first experience in the spotlight, the first time they had been allowed to compete and to win and to feel special.

Most had never been away from home, traveled in an airplane, or attended a banquet or dance, not to mention losing a close finish or winning a medal. Yet they conducted themselves in a manner that amazed and pleased their parents, teachers, and coaches and gratified the people of the Kennedy Foundation who had believed in them all the while.

No athletic competition had ever been the scene of such friendship and good will. Athletic contests are often described in terms of the "thrill of victory and the agony of defeat." In this contest there was no agony, and the thrill was not just in winning but in competing as well. While the concepts of winning and losing were understood by the participants, those who did not win were happy to have crossed the finish line, and they were intent upon practicing more and improving their skills. No one who attended that first Special Olympics Games could fail to realize that they were worthwhile.

During a national press conference held during the games, Eunice Kennedy Shriver emphasized the reasons behind them:

> Today's Special Olympics Games have not been organized as a spectacle. They are not being conducted just for fun. The Special Olympics prove a very fundamental fact. The fact that exceptional children—retarded children—can be exceptional athletes. The fact that through sports they can realize their potential for growth. . . . Our purpose here today is to secure a pledge that *all* retarded children will have this chance in the future. . . .

Mrs. Shriver also announced that the Foundation was pledging $75,000 to underwrite, in 1969, local, state, or regional Special Olympics in communities that wished to follow Chicago's lead, and continued financial support for International Special Olympics Games to be held every two years hence.

National response to the Chicago games was greater than the foundation had hoped. The event had received excellent press coverage, and a number of national, state, and local organizations were eager to become involved in future games. Those states that had been represented at Chicago were "hooked," so to speak, for coaches, chaperons, and participants alike had returned with glowing reports of the experience. Many states not represented were eager to take part in subsequent games.

Faced with this response, the Kennedy Foundation realized that a strong central organization was needed to provide direction, standardization of rules and procedures, and generally to oversee the programs in various states. Shortly after the International Special Olympics in Chicago Senator Edward Kennedy, president of the Kennedy Foundation, announced the formation of Special Olympics, Inc., with Eunice Kennedy Shriver as president. Its stated purpose was to serve as a framework for physical education, recreation, and sports activities, to increase the quality and quantity of physical education activities for all retarded citizens, and eventually to make Olympics training a special part of the regular school program for the retarded.

The seven-member board of directors heading Special Olympics, Inc., had a variety of responsibilities. One of its first undertakings was a massive public education campaign whose purpose was not only to inform the public of the program but also to educate the public regarding the capabilities of the retarded and the need for sports programs for them. The campaign was also designed to encourage financial and volunteer support.

Equally as important as gaining such support was keeping it. Special Olympics, Inc., aware that a high degree of organization was necessary to make the program a success, developed and disseminated Special Olympics training materials and determined rules and guidelines for establishing Special Olympics programs, selecting participants, raising funds, and organizing meets. Eventually, Special Olympics, Inc., even provided sample medical release and parental consent forms in order that such forms be standardized to cover all exigencies; and medals, medallions, and ribbons were to be obtained through the Foundation in order to reduce costs and ensure that these symbols would be uniform throughout the country and thus more meaningful.

In addition, Special Olympics, Inc., provided for research and evaluation of the program, not only to justify it but also to provide future direction. State and area directors were asked to submit detailed reports on activities in their respective areas, and beginning in March 1969, annual conferences were held at which Special Olympics, Inc., personnel and state and area directors could exchange ideas, evaluate past performances, and discuss plans for the future.

Gradually, the organizational structures and guidelines established by Special Olympics, Inc., became firmly rooted, and the program acquired strength and permanency. By 1970, state and area directors were taking on much more responsibility, and they in turn were developing stronger volunteer staffs and attracting more permanent funding sources.

The Special Olympics program has flourished. From its beginnings at Chicago's Soldier Field where 1,000 young people from twenty-four states plus Washington, D.C., and Canada participated, the program has grown so remarkably that in 1975 it could boast a list of impressive statistics. In that year over 15,000 training programs and local, area, and state meets were held and 65,000 retarded people participated in State Games; 150,000 volunteers contributed their time and energy to nearly every aspect of the program. Altogether there were some 500,000 mentally retarded children and adults participating in training programs and meets. Every state in the Union is now represented, as well as the District of Columbia; and Australia, Hong Kong, the Bahamas, Canada, Mexico, Germany, France, Belgium, Brazil, El Salvador, and the Philippines are firmly committed to the program. The goal is to establish the Special Olympics program in at least twenty foreign countries, including the Soviet Union.

Special Olympics, Inc., is pleased with the success of the Special Olympics program but emphasizes that there is still much to be done. Despite the impressive statistics, actually only about 15 per cent of the nation's retarded population are involved, and of this number far too many receive training only a few weeks before the games. The goal of Special Olympics, Inc., is a year-round athletic training program *focused* on the Special Olympics Games, not consisting almost solely of the games. Still, Special Olympics, Inc., does not underrate the importance of the games, for it is the games that have commanded national attention and attracted national support for the program as a whole. It is the games that were the subject of the gravest misgivings back in 1968, and it is at the games that, year after year, Special Olympians have proved those early misgivings groundless.

One of the initial questions concerned how well the retarded could be expected to perform in athletic events. While the aim of the Special Olympics is not to train its young participants for eventual competition with people of normal intelligence, the outstanding performances of some Special Olympians have nevertheless served to vindicate the belief that given proper training some retarded people are capable of remarkable accomplishments, even when compared to those of higher intelligence. In the 1970 International Special Olympics, Julius Shackleford of Stroudsburg, Pennsylvania, and Earl Britt of Parsons, Kansas, tied for the gold medal in the high jump at 5 feet 10 inches. In 1896, a jump of 5 feet 10 inches won a silver medal in the regular Olympic Games. Again in 1970, Perry Clegg of Mexia, Texas, ran the mile in 4 minutes, 54 seconds, only 14.6 seconds slower than the gold medal-winning 1,500-meter decathlon performance in the 1968 regular Olympic Games. The accomplishments of some of the other Special Olympics record holders are equally impressive. But the aim of the Special Olympics is not to set records; it is to give the retarded the opportunity for new experiences of success and new feelings of achievement.

A common misapprehension was that the participants would not be able to cope with the unfamiliar surroundings at State or International games and that the stressful situation would prove harmful to them. It has been found that, on the contrary, most of the participants thrive in their new surroundings. The trip to another city and actually staying overnight away from home or institution are as exciting as the games themselves. When fifteen-year-old Mark Kelsey, who was born with Downs' Syndrome, or Mongolism, learned that he was going to the 1974 Tennessee Special Olympics at Nashville, he spent days practicing saying "Nashville."

Competitors in the Indiana Special Olympics in 1974 were boarded in dormitories at Indiana State University, Terre Haute, and the experience of staying in the dorms, "like the college kids" or "like the big boys," was memorable. Asked to write about the games, few of the participants failed to mention their dormitory experience:

> I like to go stay at nigth.

> It is fun to stay all nigth at the olypics.
> I like to dance and eat the goad food.
> Taking showers was lots of fun ther.

> I like my on room and staying all night.

> . . . and I stayed at the dorms, stayed all
> night at the dorms.
> I like to take a
> bath in shower.
> I ike to eat there.

> I like to take a shower at
> the special olympics and eat
> and sleep. . . .

Meeting new people, far from being stressful for most of the athletes, was thrilling. The Indiana Special Olympics Committee sponsored dances for the participants, which the girls, in particular, remember with pleasure.

At the 1972 International Special Olympics, held at UCLA, Charles Grant, athletic supervisor at Rosewood School in Baltimore, Maryland, was not sure how the children he accompanied to the games would react in social situations. "We knew what these kids could do on an athletic level but not on a social one. It was like a learning process for all who went. To watch these kids go up to children from different states, introduce themselves, and carry on conversations was incredible. We didn't know how they would perform socially but I think most of them did at least as well as they did athletically."

Sometimes, the social situation at Special Olympics Games is easier for the participants to deal with than social situations in their home towns. Ralphie Crawson, a fifteen-year-old from Silver Springs, Maryland, found this to be true at UCLA in 1972. He was very large for his age at 6 feet 2 inches and 190 pounds. He also had a speech impediment. All his life, kids had made fun of him. But no one made fun of him at UCLA. Ralphie, who at birth was not expected ever to be able to run, ran the 50-yard dash in less than nine seconds and became quite a celebrity among the other participants.

While the excitement of new surroundings and new people is an important aspect of the Special Olympics Games experience, it is in the events themselves that the participants can show their abilities and satisfy their desire to compete. Over the years, the Kennedy Foundation has established a number of guidelines to make the games effective and enjoyable for the participants.

The program aims to reach as many people as possible, and adults as well as young people are welcome. In general, any mentally retarded person aged eight and over who has an IQ of 75 or under is eligible, and this rule is flexible. For example, if every child in a class qualifies but one, who has an IQ of 80, then of course he is included. The one really firm rule is that the entrant must be *mentally* retarded, not just physically or emotionally handicapped. The reason is that Special Olympics is still not reaching enough of the mentally retarded who could and should participate. Opening the program to those with other handicaps would overburden the existing program. Once Special Olympics has reached all or most of the mentally retarded, to whom it is committed, then it is conceivable that categories for other handicapped people will be developed.

The number of Special Olympics events has been increased greatly since 1968, in order to give more retarded persons a chance to compete. Before the Special Olympics began, the Kennedy Foundation was not certain that mentally retarded persons could take part in more than a limited number of simple games geared toward individuals. Since then, the participants have proven that they are capable of considerably more sophisticated sports activity and can perform just as well in team as in individual competition. Today the games feature team events such as basketball, volleyball, floor hockey, and bowling and a greatly expanded gymnastics and swimming program.

Competition divisions at Special Olympics Games and the means of assigning participants to these divisions have been very carefully worked out. The major purpose of the guidelines developed to cover such matters, as of the games themselves, is to give the participants a feeling of being athletes rather than retarded persons. Thus, other than chronological age, the major criterion for assigning a competitor to a division is not his intelligence but his ability and his level of performance. The primary objective is to avoid situations in which some participants finish far behind the others. Sometimes, directors face the problem of having one or two entrants whose performance is so poor that they do not really belong in any of the three or four established divisions. In such cases, they are urged to resolve the problem in a way that will benefit the poorly performing participants, by creating another division or shifting division lines so that each has a realistic opportunity. Under these guidelines the chance for each entrant to win or to have a good try at it, while engaging in a really competitive situation, is increased, and this is true for the whole range of Special Olympians.

Russell, age fifteen, had not even been recognized as retarded by his teachers in his home town in Michigan. They saw him merely as a quiet boy who could not quite compete with his classmates. Not until the Special Olympics gained national attention did it occur to Russell's teachers that perhaps his inability to compete in athletics stemmed from retardation. He was tested and found to be mildly retarded and was immediately urged to participate in the Special Olympics program. Special Olympics gave him a chance to compete with others his age and ability. In 1973 he won a gold medal in tumbling at the Michigan Special Olympics Games. In 1974 he won a second gold medal.

There had never been any question that Stevie Waddell was retarded. He had been born with Downs' Syndrome. But there is a place for nearly every retarded person in the Special Olympics, and eight-year-old Stevie was no exception when he stepped to the pool at Florida Atlantic University in Boca Raton, Florida, to make the

25-yard swim in the 1974 Florida Special Olympics Games.

At the time, Special Olympics rules allowed separate categories for extremely low-functioning children. Being the only entrant in this event, Stevie was sure to win. But that did not cause him to be any less determined as he stuck out his chest, looked around at the audience, and dived into the pool. Then, in the utter joy of participating, he began to grin, and as he paddled toward the other end of the pool, his face reflected such sheer delight that no one present could have been unaffected. Soon, the entire audience was grinning and clapping and cheering, and by the time the three-foot-tall Stevie had paddled the length of the 25-yard-long pool and had been helped out, he was receiving a standing ovation. Waiting with official congratulations was Mrs. Rose Kennedy, and after she had spoken a few brief words, Stevie responded with a deep and dramatic bow. The audience applauded heartily. Stevie, aware that the first bow had gone over very well, bowed again.

Like the competitive divisions, the games themselves are structured to increase the feeling of recognition and importance of each participant. They are attended by much ceremony and contain elements that are found in the regular Olympic Games. Awards to the winners of an event are presented as soon after the event as possible, ideally, as soon as the competition is completed, for awards mean much more to the winners when presented at this time than at the end of the games. Only three medals are given for each event, but all participants receive place awards for their efforts. Often the awards are presented by VIPs—celebrities in the entertainment or sports fields. Having an award handed to him by one of his heroes means as much to a retarded person as to anyone else. Ideally, a photographer is on hand to take pictures of every presentation, in order that the participant will have not only a medal but also a picture to show proudly long after the games are over.

This sense of accomplishment is one of the primary aims of the Special Olympics. For one thing, it reinforces for the participants the importance and fun of sports activity. For another, experiencing success is particularly meaningful for the retarded, who are left behind in so many other areas in their lives, and this is true for the mildly retarded as well as the severely retarded. Russell, the boy in Michigan whose retardation was not even recognized until he was nearly fourteen years old, was so proud of his first gold medal that in the following year the ribbon holding that medal had to be replaced, so frayed had it become from the touching and stroking it received.

In the 1974 Texas Special Olympics, a more seriously retarded boy who had won a silver medal smiled so long and hard that his "mouth got tired." So he proceeded to hold the corners of his mouth up with his fingers as he walked around showing his medal. And at the International Olympics in 1972 a little girl born with Downs' Syndrome stood on the winners' platform clutching her bronze medal and repeating over and over, "I won, I won." Even though not every participant is awarded a medal on the ceremonial platform, each and every Special Olympian knows that he is loved and cared about.

Initial misgivings about Special Olympics had not involved the participants' winning but their losing. How would they react to yet another failure? A 1969 research report on the Michigan Special Olympics addressed the question, among others, of whether or not the participants feared losing and how the fear, if present, affected them. The report concluded that although about a third of the entrants did indicate some fear of losing, they were able to admit their fears in an open, rational manner. Their fears did not make them despondent, or cause them to be afraid to try. Researchers watched for signs of emotional upset. "We expected some of the kids to cry or appear downhearted. Virtually no such behaviors were observed."

Naturally, the competitors do not like to lose. Among the responses of those who participated in the 1974 Indiana Special Olympics were the following:

> I Did not lith it ot well.
> I like to winning But I Did
> not like to loose. We cane in
> secon. We did not play one tene.

> I went last year. I ran and throw
> softball. I do not like to run. I
> want to throw the softball and long
> jump this year. Dorem is fun. I did
> not like to lose. One kid ran into me
> and cause me to lose.

Certainly, these young athletes understood the concept of losing and would prefer to have won. Yet, their responses are no different from those one would expect from non-retarded persons who had lost an athletic event. Everyone wants to be a winner. Losing becomes dangerous only when one who has lost no longer wants to play the game. It is the policy of the Special Olympics to encourage trying again, and at the games, even those who do not win are given a special award of their own for making the attempt. Everyone comes away from the games with something.

Jimmy Love, of Maryland, has shown that losing need not be a debilitating experience for a retarded youngster, even when a loss in athletic competition is associated with the loss of a loved parent.

Jimmy was the only one of six students from his school who did not win a medal at the National Special Olympics in Chicago in 1970. His father had attended with the school's delegation, and naturally Jimmy had wanted to win a medal and to make his father proud of him. When his father died during the ensuing school year, Jimmy regretted his failure to win even more. Yet, Jimmy continued to practice his swimming and to work toward competing in future Special Olympics Games. Of five students from his school to go to the National Special Olympics in California in 1972, Jimmy was the only one to bring back a medal, a silver one for placing second in swimming competition. Not only did the Special Olympics program help Jimmy to become a winner, but also, through the training he was given, it provided him the attention and guidance he needed for his emotional development. By 1974 he had won numerous medals in local contests and eleven in state meets.

Quite obviously, the misgivings expressed about the Special Olympics Games have been disproven by Special Olympians who have participated in the games. Certainly it is possible to find negative reactions and experiences, on the part of both participants and parents:

> I just do not like to go because many people make fun of you. I do not like to be in the newspaper. And well I think it is dumb and it embarrasses me. I feel like you are retarded.

> I would like to go really but my mom said that it is full with strange looking people. Last year I went and it was fun. I am sorry about this year.

But for every negative reaction to the games there are a score of positive reactions, not just from the participants but from the observers as well. There was the 300-yard race in the 1972 Iowa Special Olympics in which two girls had been running together for nearly the entire race when one realized they were approaching the finish line. She increased her speed, but when the other girl tried to do the same she tripped and fell down. The first girl saw this, and, rather than continuing on to cross the finish line, she returned to help her friend. There was the state meet when a boy ran his race on crutches and another meet where a blind child followed the voice of his coach around the track and across the finish line.

And there was the girl who won the 25-yard butterfly event in the California Special Olympics Games in 1973. She stood on the highest of the three raised platforms, flanked by those who had placed second and third in the event. The judge approached. In his hand she saw the yellow gleam of a medal—her medal. Suddenly, she was squealing and laughing. "My God!" cried her mother, rushing forward. "My little girl—it's the first sound she's ever made!"

Chapter II: A Grass Roots Movement

In 1968, some one thousand retarded youngsters participated in the International Special Olympics in Chicago. By 1975 there were few states in which there were not at least one thousand participants in the State Games alone, and, over all, some five hundred thousand retarded persons were involved. The growth of the Special Olympics program has been phenomenal, and much of the credit is due to committed individuals who have been willing to work on a volunteer basis to further the cause of sports training for the retarded. Now, in every state there exists a strong and well-organized State Special Olympics Committee, which maintains close contact with the Joseph P. Kennedy, Jr., Foundation and Special Olympics, Inc.

Indiana has one of the most successful Special Olympics programs in the country, but like the Special Olympics program itself, it began on a very small scale. Judy Campbell and Thomas Songster, teachers at Indiana State University at Terre Haute, and former codirectors of the Indiana Special Olympics, were involved in the state program from the very beginning.

"In 1968," Judy Campbell recalls, "I had just come out of graduate school and had gotten a job as physical fitness director for the Association of Retarded Children [ARC] in Terre Haute. There was a very dynamic lady in the city, a local television personality, named Helen Ryan, who knew people at the Kennedy Foundation and who received a communiqué about the first Special Olympics Games to be held in Chicago that summer. And then I saw an article about the Special Olympics in the AAHPR [American Alliance for Health, Physical Education and Recreation] Journal. Helen Ryan said to me, 'We should have a team,' and that summer at the ARC camp I began to train the kids. We trained them all summer and we took ten of them to the first International Games in Chicago in 1968. There were thirty children from Indiana that year, and we had brought ten. That was the beginning."

By 1969, Special Olympics, Inc., had been established, and each interested state was to have its own games. In Indiana, the Association for Retarded Children took on the task of organizing the games. Judy Campbell served as co-ordinator for the Terre Haute area and took a large number of children to the State Games, which were held at Bush Stadium at Indianapolis.

"But Indianapolis, or the Bush Stadium at Indianapolis, was a difficult site for the games because it lacked
the proper facilities," Judy Campbell recalls. "There
were not sufficient housing accommodations, and we had
to stay in a hotel some distance from the games and be
bused back and forth to Bush Stadium. They did not have
a track that could accommodate the 300-yard run, just not
the proper facilities. By this time I was working at Indiana State University at Terre Haute, and I opened my
mouth and said, 'Why don't we have the next games at
our university?'"

What Judy Campbell proposed was easier said than
done. A considerable sum of money would have to be
raised to make the proposition financially feasible, but she
and others at the university, among them Thomas
Songster, were willing to try. The two were elected
codirectors of the newly formed State Special Olympics
Committee.

"We started with nothing," says Judy Campbell,
"didn't have one cent. We didn't have enough money for
stamps or paper to do a mailing asking for funds for the
games. But we got the money for the mailing, and as a result of the mailing we raised enough money to be able to
bring the games here to Terre Haute. When you look at
how successful our program is now it is hard to believe
what we started with."

"Things really began to get going when we moved the
games here to Terre Haute," says Thomas Songster. "We
organized committees, and we began to send representatives to various special education and physical education conventions to try to get those people interested in

the program. We went out to the schools, to try to get them involved; but that was slow going at first. Many of the parents had just been persuaded to place their retarded youngsters in special schools and special classes a year or two before. They had just gotten used to that idea, and then suddenly they were confronted with the Special Olympics Games. That was a whole new story. Their children would have to be away from home for two or three days, in a strange setting. The idea frightened them and they were very hesitant."

Songster and Campbell expected many of the teachers of the retarded to be hesitant, too. After all, asking them to become involved with Special Olympics was asking them to take on considerable additional work. It would be their responsibility to see that parental consent forms and medical release forms were signed, to convince school officials to support the program, to let them use the schools' athletic facilities, to allow the children time out from other activities in order to practice. It would be their job to train the children, to raise the funds to go to the games, to accompany the children to the games.

Surprisingly, however, many teachers were eager to take on the additional work. These teachers felt strongly that the mentally retarded were being shortchanged in the area of physical education. There were many programs for physical rehabilitation of the physically handicapped, opportunities not available to the mentally retarded.

"Those who were teachers in schools for the retarded were very receptive," says Tom Songster, "and they became very energetic participants. They had great spirit.

THE STORY OF
THE SPECIAL OLYMPICS

1. Fort Lewis Army Base personnel add color and excitement to the opening parade at the 1974 Washington Special Olympics.

2. Dressed alike and displaying identifying banners, young athletes march in the opening parade at Kansas Special Olympics Games.

3. A young athlete completes the standing long jump in
Kansas Special Olympics competition.

4. "Let me win, but if I cannot win, let me be brave in the attempt" — the motto of the Special Olympics.

5. Winners in bowling competition at the 1974 Washington Special Olympics Games pose with Mrs. William B. Fulton in one of the recreational facilities at Fort Lewis Army Base.

6. When a military base such as Fort Lewis plays host to Special Olympics Games, military personnel make up a large proportion of the volunteer work force.

like the dorm
t is fun. We eat
here. It is so fun We
ike it. — We are going
gain. The olympics
s fun it is. We slep
here

7. At the 1974 Indiana Special Olympics Games, participants were especially enthusiastic about staying in the
dormitories at Indiana State University.

8. Eunice Kennedy Shriver and other members of the Kennedy family attend as many State Games as possible, and wherever they go they work hard — encouraging youngsters as they compete, helping to conduct clinics, and generally showing the young athletes how much they care.

The first year we had a basketball tournament I remember getting very upset, at first, about how the coaches were acting. They were screaming and shouting, and I was getting angry. And then I realized, my God, they're acting just like regular coaches and that's what they should be doing. The spirit is fantastic, and so many teachers of the retarded are eager to take on all the hassles involved because they are really committed to the program. And they are helping to change the attitudes of the parents with their positive attitude.

"The attitudes are changing in the public schools as well," Songster continues. "While previously the kids in special education classes were just put there and forgotten, now attempts are being made to do more for them. Last year, one of my former students was a first-year teacher in a poor, ghetto school in Indianapolis. She had been involved with Special Olympics here at the university and she urged the principal to get the special classes involved. The principal was apprehensive, but finally she got him and some of the other teachers interested. They began to train the children to prepare to go to the State Games; they planned to take forty-eight to fifty kids. Then they found out that it would cost forty dollars for each child to go to the games. Naturally, the children's parents didn't have money for that sort of thing.

"She brought the matter to the school authorities, and in typical bureaucratic style the school refused to allow fund-raising activities in the name of the school for this purpose. So she brought the matter to the faculty, and all of a sudden the teachers began to see that the special education children were worthy of having this chance. They raised enough money to send forty-six children to the State Games.

"As luck would have it, two of her children happened to be in the first race of the 50-yard dash. There were those forty-four other kids standing there watching those two run the first race of the games for them, and the two kids came in first and second. Well, the enthusiasm in that group, from that time on, was unbelievable. On Monday morning, back at school, they were the honored guests at a special school assembly. They were no longer mentally retarded kids but the winners at Special Olympics."

As the Special Olympics program gained support from parents and teachers of the retarded, the Indiana State Special Olympics Committee found itself in need of greater financial help. "By 1971," says Tom Songster, "we had become more sophisticated, and we incorporated as a non-profit educational foundation, which, for example, entitles people to give us money on a tax deductible basis."

Today, while the Indiana Special Olympics program can always use more money, it is one of the most financially secure programs in the country. "Each year we get a grant from the Kennedy Foundation of about a thousand dollars," says Judy Campbell, "because we are such an active program. Then, on the state level, the Tri-Kappa Sororities give us about a thousand on a yearly basis, and last year they gave fifteen hundred. Then, each club across the state gives various donations to its area committee or to us. Businesses, clubs, service clubs, the newspapers, television networks—they all give something.

"We're given little things that in reality are very big. Equipment, services. We don't pay for any services. People volunteer—the nurses, the office staff, the band, the people who run the events at meets."

The students in Tom Songster's classes volunteer to work in the program, and in fact the course he teaches during the first summer term each year is called Physical Education for Special Olympics.

"It takes so much work to get everything done," Songster explains. "For example, holding two hundred ten heats of the 50-yard dash. We have to have a hundred sixty-five volunteers to run the events, so you know that somewhere along the line we have to pick up a lot of other people."

The members of the Indiana Special Olympics Committee have clearly been successful in mobilizing the people of Indiana to support the Special Olympics program. Yet, despite massive co-operation from nearly every segment of the state's population, the heaviest responsibilities fall upon the shoulders of the committee members, particularly the directors, who spend perhaps twice as much time working on Special Olympics matters than at their salaried jobs.

In June, 1974, the committee learned that a grant requested from the Eli Lilly Foundation had been approved and that over a two-and-a-half-year period they would receive $128,500. It was a direct grant for administrative services. It would make possible the hiring of a full-time state director and a full-time secretary as well as the establishment of a Special Olympics office. It would also make possible more publicity on the local level and, it was hoped, greater participation in the program throughout the state. Although there are no precise statistics on the total retarded population of Indiana, Campbell and Songster estimate that perhaps 10 to 15 per cent of retarded youngsters of school age are participating in the Special Olympics program, although older retarded people are certainly not excluded. The oldest participant at the 1974 games was fifty-eight, and at the 1973 games a fifty-three-year-old won a medal. The Indiana Special Olympics people would like to see 100 per cent participation, and they are hopeful that money from the Lilly grant can be used to come closer to this goal.

"I don't think there's any limit to what Special Olympics can do," says Tom Songster, "and I think it will prove to have a great impact not only on the retarded but on the non-retarded as well. Physical education laws in Indiana are weak and ineffective. We're going to have some new laws. We're going to have some effects here that will cause people to start thinking that non-retarded children need some help, too. Some day we'll have better programs for normal kids who are not well co-ordinated or who are not physically fit—not necessarily Special Olympics-type programs but good, sound physical education programs."

Chapter III: A Program for Fitness: Much More Than the Games Themselves

International Special Olympics Games were held in 1968, 1970, and 1972, but beginning in 1975, they were to be held every four years, like the regular Olympic Games. State Games are held during the spring and summer months each year. The State and International games receive a great amount of publicity, to the extent that a large segment of the American public is under the misapprehension that the Special Olympics program comprises only these State and International games. Actually, the emphasis of the Special Olympics program is not on the games themselves but on the training and activity that is involved in preparation for the games. The games are merely a forum to display the results of this training and a means for rewarding and reinforcing the importance of the training for the participants as well as for their coaches, teachers, and parents.

Year-round sport activity and physical training of the retarded is not yet a reality in many areas of the United States, even in those areas where participation in the Special Olympics Games is high. Too often, training of a participant in the games is given only a few weeks or a few months prior to the games, after which the training ceases until the advent of the next year's games. The aim of the Kennedy Foundation is that the Special Olympics program be a year-round program, culminating in, rather than consisting chiefly of, the formal contests. It is still a distant goal, but it is hoped that with continued effort on the part of those committed to the Special Olympics program, the State and International games will assume their proper proportion in the over-all program, as merely the frosting on a substantial cake of regular physical activity for the mentally retarded.

The chief philosophy behind the Special Olympics program is that physical activity is as necessary for retarded persons as it is for the non-retarded and that such activity can cause improvement not only in health, physical appearance, and co-ordination but also in behavior in school or on the job. The correctness of this approach has been proven by studies not directly related to the Special Olympics program.

For example, in a Texas study concerning the effects of regular physical activity on retarded children, all the teachers interviewed noted marked improvement in classroom work habits and performance of children who had participated in the sports program. Most importantly, they noticed that the children would try and actually do successfully many things that they formerly believed were impossible—both of an intellectual and motor nature.

In 1973, officials in the Boston public schools reported that the number of retarded children in special classes who had been able to return to regular classes had more than doubled since daily physical education had been added to their curriculum three years before.

Part of the reason why retarded people are so "different" in appearance from the rest of society is that they lack co-ordination and they show it, physically. Not until well into this century did the realization occur that the peculiar awkward and unco-ordinated appearance of the retarded might be due to the fact that no one had ever attempted to teach them grace and co-ordination, which are not necessarily natural attributes of the human race. A child reared by wolves would likely run on all fours and acquire many of the mannerisms of wolves. A retarded child reared in an institution for the retarded will imitate the movements and mannerisms of those around him. Even a retarded child who is brought up at home will not necessarily acquire muscle co-ordination unless someone helps him to do so.

Thus, David Basquin, who was born with Downs' Syndrome and had a physical defect as well, was unco-ordinated and physically underdeveloped even though he lived at home and had caring and interested parents. A disease of the hipbone had caused one of his legs to be shorter than the other, and because he had not received

regular athletic training his muscles in general were underdeveloped.

By 1969, David, then age twelve, was enrolled in the
Mentally Handicapped Program at Blackhawk Park in
Chicago; and through that program he became involved
in the Special Olympics. At his first Special Olympics
Games, in 1970, he entered the 25-yard freestyle and
25-yard backstroke events and won a ribbon and a bronze
medal. In each succeeding year his speed increased by at
least three or four seconds and he won more and more
ribbons and medals, which he proudly exhibits to everyone who visits. But David's swimming speed is not the
only thing that has improved. "His co-ordination and
concentration are better," his father says; "even in school
all his crafts projects are improved. He's made over fifty
of them now. . . . He knows new words now, and knows
what they mean, especially things like 'freestyle' and
'guard.' He even knows to start with the gun. When he
first began to swim he would watch the one next to him
and when the other went, David went. Now he doesn't
need that any more. . . . Believe it or not, David could
never jump or swing on the swings in his whole life. He
can do both those things now. He even reads a little."

Joseph Moody, a fourteen-year-old boy in Michigan,
was also born with Downs' Syndrome. He was always fat
and rather sluggish until he became involved in the Special Olympics program. The teachers at the Richfield
School in Flint, Michigan, which Joe attended, began in
the fall of 1973 to train students for the 1974 Michigan
Special Olympics, and they did not choose just the stu-

dents whom they felt could do well in sports. Instead, they trained all the students.

At first, Joe was reluctant to participate in the training, which involved running and jumping. Being so heavy, he found it very hard to run; he would be breathless after just a few yards. And jumping seemed far beyond his abilities. It was quite obvious that Joe needed to go on a diet, and with the co-operation of his mother he was placed on one.

As training progressed, and as he lost weight, Joe also lost his reluctance to participate. He began to excel in small ways, managing to run in place longer than the other students and being able to jump farther almost on a weekly basis. Eventually, he was able to do all the exercises listed in the *Special Olympics Training Manual*.

Meanwhile, Joe's family began to take a new interest in him. His older brother, active in track and field at his own high school, began to run with Joe in the neighborhood, and when Joe participated in the area meet he proudly wore his brother's track suit. In just one year, Joe's self-confidence increased tremendously. Slimmer now, and better co-ordinated, he is more self-confident than he has ever been before. Academically, too, he is more self-assured, able to do his schoolwork with greater independence. In the past, he constantly went to his teachers seeking explanations of the work. Of course, this was partly due to his short attention span; unable to concentrate on one thing for very long, he would go to his teachers for relief more than with serious questions. By the spring of 1974, however, he could remain at his academic work twice as long as he could the previous fall.

Improvement in attention span is one of the most remarkable effects of regular physical activity, which trains the mind as well as the body. For many retarded youngsters, sitting through an entire meal, for example, even when one is very hungry, is impossible. Linda, a Chicago girl whose brain was damaged at the age of three months by meningitis, had, as a child, to be strapped to a chair in order to finish a meal. As a teen-ager, her attention span was only a few seconds until she became involved in the Special Olympics program. The 300-yard run takes almost a full minute. Before her training, Linda would have been incapable of the concentration needed to complete the run. Yet in 1970 and 1971 she won second and third place, respectively, in that event at the State Games.

For retarded persons, because of shortness of attention span, physical activity involves not only great physical exertion but great emotional expenditure as well. Brian Loeb, at age sixteen, was considered to have the intellectual ability of an eight-year-old and to be unable to advance beyond that level. Physically, his level of performance was even lower. When Brian became involved in a program of physical activity with concentration upon swimming, even the simplest strokes seemed too much for him to learn. He had neither the physical ability nor the attention span to swim the length of the pool. Yet, within two years, from 1971 to 1973, he became a Special Olympics champion at the backstroke, freestyle, and relay. Today, he could easily swim a mile.

Improved physical performance leads to improved academic and job performance, and this is true for the severely retarded as well as the mildly retarded. Joe

Moody, whose co-ordination improved so much from physical training and diet, also improved in his academic work, even though he suffered from Downs' Syndrome. Kyle Hansen, a thirteen-year-old who lives in Utah, was tested in 1970 and found to be retarded, with his performance score significantly lower than his verbal score. He was put into a program of extended physical education centered around the Special Olympics, and when he was retested in January 1974, he showed improvement in every area, with impressive gains in verbal, performance, and full-scale tests. While many factors were involved in this improvement, his teachers give a substantial amount of credit to the Special Olympics program. They also credit the extended program of physical activity in which Kyle has participated with helping his parents better accept Kyle's situation. Kyle's parents, especially his father, blamed themselves for his intellectual handicap. Now, seeing that Kyle can indeed improve and watching him compete in, and win, athletic contests, Mr. and Mrs. Hansen have a new pride in their son.

The Special Olympics also changed the home life of Kenneth McIntyre of Maine. Kenneth had gone to special schools for years, and his parents, initially ashamed of him, had over the years become resigned to his condition. In 1971, Kenneth, a non-reader who could do no math and whose verbal ability was poorly developed, became involved in the Special Olympics program, and in his first local competition he won three first-place ribbons in the 50-yard and 300-yard runs and in the relay event as well as a second-place ribbon in the mile run. Later in the summer, he won a gold medal in volleyball at the Maine

State Games. His success at the two meets caused Kenneth to take a greater interest in his academic work, for the one success made the idea of success in other areas possible.

As Kenneth won more medals in the 1972 Maine Special Olympics and was selected to represent Maine in the International Special Olympics in California, his academic performance continued to improve. He was taken from his special school and enrolled in Rockland High School. In June 1974, he graduated from the high school right along with the non-retarded graduating seniors. Kenneth now reads well, does math, and is more verbally skilled than he was in 1971. He is a confident young man and a happy one, for not only has he proved to himself that he can succeed but he has proved it to his parents as well. Once doubtful of his abilities, Kenneth's parents are now very, very proud of their son.

Ann Prothero's retardation is mild. Yet her problem was sufficient to cause her parents to look for help, and there was a serious question whether or not she would be able to function in a regular school situation. She was enrolled in several programs designed to help the mildly retarded, and while these programs may have contributed to her development, not until she became involved in a physical activity program geared toward participation in the Special Olympics was this development really apparent. Her father, Marshall Prothero, reported in early 1974:

> "I believe the training, the travel (independent of
> Mom and Daddy), and finally *winning* something did
> more for her than anything else. She has since shown

a greater interest in school. She completed the driver's education course and passed all the tests at the Bureau of Motor Vehicles without a mistake. This has given additional independence to her and higher gas bills to us. She has had a minor accident and handled herself by the book. She now holds down a part-time job while going to school and is about as well adjusted as we could expect—better than some of our other children."

Unlike Kyle Hansen and Ann Prothero, David, a twenty-one-year-old from Chicago was declared severely retarded when he was seven years old. The prognosis went on to say, "It is not felt that he will be able to be educated. . . . in our opinion, he will never be self-supporting." With the help of the Special Olympics program, this prognosis has been proven wrong. One of the youths who have been involved in the Special Olympics from the beginning, David has entered every event since the meets were conceived. And the longer he has participated, the more he has improved. While in 1968 he completed the 300-yard run in 2 minutes 30 seconds, in 1971 he made the run in 56 seconds! His physical co-ordination improved; his attention span increased. The young man who in 1962 was expected never to be self-supporting landed a forty-hour-a-week job running errands at a Chicago photo company. Being self-supporting did not cause David to lose his interest in physical activity. "Every night," he says, "I run home from the bus stop because I know I have to keep physically fit."

Lorna Jean, age sixteen, learned to read and write as a result of the Special Olympics program. In school in

Michigan she was such a discipline problem that in 1970 school authorities refused to allow her to return. She was so violent and self-destructive that in May of the same year she was brought up before a judge who was to decide whether or not she should be permanently institutionalized. The judge looked skeptical when Lorna Jean's mother pleaded that her daughter was simply restless and energetic and that if they could just find the right school Lorna Jean would be all right. Still, he was sympathetic, and he agreed to let Lorna Jean's mother travel to Chicago and try to find a program that would accept her.

The program Lorna Jean's mother found was deeply committed to physical activity and training for the Special Olympics, and, after only a few days there, a change began to occur in Lorna Jean. She responded well to the athletics program, and with the Special Olympics Games in mind she channeled her restless energy toward that goal. Her behavior problems lessened.

Then came the Special Olympics, Lorna's first. She won three medals, and it was then that she, herself, decided to go to school to learn to read and write. Shortly thereafter, Lorna participated in a Chicago Water Festival and was selected to represent her team on the Water Festival Yacht. There she met a young man who was about her age, and during the time they were on the yacht together, she discovered that he could write his name. Lorna Jean could only print. She vowed that the next time she went anywhere, she would be able to write.

Since then, Lorna Jean has learned to write, at least well enough to be understood, and to read simple words

and paragraphs. "Her teacher says she's 100 per cent better than two years ago," said Lorna Jean's mother in 1974.
"She's really trying to learn—doesn't want to hurt anyone."

Part of the reason why the Special Olympics Games are
so well-publicized is that they are often the scene of
human dramas that touch even those who otherwise are
"put off" by the retarded. Yet, while there are fewer dramatic incidents in the day-to-day or week-to-week physical activity and training that is the aim of the Special
Olympics program, there is drama here as well, not just
the drama of a day but the drama of a year or many
years.

There is the drama of nineteen-year-old Jill Shea from
Chicago. She had a history of brain seizures and she was
also an almost totally non-emotional child who had never
laughed or cried. Early in 1970, she began to participate
in a program of regular physical activity, centered around
the Special Olympics. As she particularly enjoyed swimming, she was encouraged to practice as often as possible.

In 1970, at the International Special Olympics, Jill won
a gold medal in the backstroke and a silver medal in
freestyle swimming, even though it was the first time she
had ever competed in an athletic event. Then in the winter of 1970 she was wracked by two massive brain seizures, and no one expected that she would ever be able to
compete in the Special Olympics Games again.

Jill had experienced such seizures before in her life,
and had suffered brain damage from them. But no additional damage was found after her two seizures in 1970.

What could be the reason for the change? Jill's medicine was the same, her lifestyle had not changed drastically over the years. The one new factor was the Special Olympics program under which, since the spring of 1970, she had participated in regular physical activity and had practiced her swimming at every possible opportunity.

It was a year and a half before Jill again participated in Special Olympics competition, for the two seizures necessitated a long period of recuperation. Exercise and swimming were a part of that recuperation, and she was slated to enter the backstroke event in the 1972 Illinois Special Olympics. She had worked hard, both physically and emotionally, to be able to compete, and as she waited her turn in the pool the excitement and tension overwhelmed her and she broke into tears. It was the first time in her life she had ever been able to cry.

Jill won the gold medal in the backstroke event, and when she heard she had been selected to go to the International Games in California she cried for the second time in her life. Thus, the Special Olympics program helped Jill Shea in two ways. Regular exercise had strengthened her and had possibly helped her body to resist the debilitating effects of the seizures. The excitement of the games and her triumph in returning to them when everything had been against it had caused her to show real emotion for the first time. A person who can cry can also learn to laugh, and the person who can laugh and cry is on the way to a more normal emotional life.

The Special Olympics program still has a long way to go toward reaching the goal of full participation by the retarded, just as the country has a long way to go in granting the retarded their right to membership in our society. One of the main problems earmarked by Special Olympics, Inc., is the lack of participation by retarded persons from certain minority groups, such as Indians and Mexican Americans. Some committees in states where this problem exists have special co-ordinators whose function is to encourage minority participation in the Special Olympics program.

In the state of Washington, which has a very active and multifaceted Special Olympics program, a foundation grant has enabled the State Special Olympics Committee to hire Dave Anderson as a Special Olympics co-ordinator, the only paid position on the committee.

"The state committee," said Anderson in 1974, "has noticed for the past few years that there have been only a few minority people involved in the program, and they wanted to know why. My job is to find out why, and to try to do something about it. Of course, my interest is not only greater minority participation but greater participation for all retarded persons in the state."

Reaching many retarded people requires crossing a great number of barriers—social, cultural, geographic, and economic.

"Retardation is more accepted among poor people of all races," Anderson says. "While the problem with middle-class parents is to get them to let their retarded child out of the closet, so to speak, the problem with lower-class parents, or families of different cultural background, is getting them to recognize that their child is retarded and that something can be done for the child."

Nowhere is the lack of programs for the retarded more

notable than among American Indians. "Indians have an entirely different cultural attitude than other Americans," says Anderson. "To them, a retarded person is said to be sacred and he is treated as sacred. I have visited Indian communities, attended their festivities, but it is hard to convince them that retarded persons need special help.

"I attended a seminar in South Dakota this past winter, and we went to a reservation in the state and organized an association for retarded children. This was only the second such association to be established on an Indian reservation in this country. But we can see that progress is being made. Eight different Indian nations were represented at that seminar: Arizona, New Mexico, Washington, South Dakota, and Nebraska all sent representatives. We are attempting to start an association for retarded children among the Indians in Washington, and we can see progress here, too. We have some Indian youngsters participating in the Special Olympics program, although the number is not as large as we would like it to be."

Special Olympics, Inc., has concentrated on developing new and better Indian programs in all states with substantial Indian populations, and participation has increased markedly.

In Washington, Anderson is also concerned with encouraging greater black participation. "One of the problems among poor blacks," says Anderson, "is that a lot of the retardation is not socially recognized. It is easier to get co-operation from parents with severely retarded children than from parents whose children are only mildly retarded. I have hope that fairly soon we can get past the barriers that prevent these children from being helped.

"The whole matter of definition constitutes a greater problem than it should, and this is true for all races. The schools help to maintain this problem at times. The word *retarded* has a stigma attached to it, and the schools tend to use euphemisms. So when you go into a school to speak, and mention the word *retarded*, you're likely to get the response, 'They're not retarded; they're mentally handicapped.' So it's a word game.

"The schools, however, are showing great progress," said Anderson in the early summer of 1974. "There are many that have never been involved in Special Olympics before that are now really interested. We've asked the principals to call all their teachers in, and in August I will be going around the state speaking to these groups of teachers, telling them what the Special Olympics is about and how it can benefit their classes and their students. In many areas there are already Special Olympics boards that can help these schools to organize their programs, and new boards will be established in areas where they have not been previously. We're getting a lot of local groups to sponsor these boards in particular regions. This way everyone is organized and on top of everything.

"We have the structure, the organizational apparatus. We have a year-round physical fitness program. I couldn't possibly name all of the programs we have in operation throughout the state. The problem is to get participation, to break down the stigma that is attached to retardation. Progress is slow, but it is evident. Since last year, we've had a 24 per cent increase in minority participation, and we intend to do better next year."

Clearly, the state of Washington is doing much to recognize and provide for its entire retarded population. In other states across the country Special Olympics Committees are actively encouraging the same.

Chapter IV: Special Olympics Games: Models of Organization and Community Co-operation

International, State, and Area Special Olympics Games follow the same basic pattern set at the first Special Olympics in 1968. The aim then, as subsequently, was to make the games a rewarding, exciting experience for the participants. The Kennedy Foundation and Special Olympics, Inc., are as firm on this as on any other aspect of the program. While it is acknowledged that local meets cannot include all the elements of International Games, State Games are expected to be similar in as many respects as possible to International Games, but on a smaller scale; and State Special Olympics Committees see to it that such expectations are met. The games are well organized, well run, and brimming with ceremony—to give the participants the spotlight, to make it *their* day or *their* weekend.

The participants arrive by bus or plane or private car the afternoon before the games begin and register at Special Olympics headquarters. They are proud to wear the name tag and special identifying ribbon or badge, for these symbols mean that they belong, that they are part of this new and exciting experience. They are in the Olympic Village, and they know it is a special place to be, a place where only they and their fellow competitors and chaperons will stay. They are ushered into their rooms and introduced to their roommates and next-door neighbors for the weekend—other participants they know and new ones to get to know. They watch intently, taking everything in—the halls, the rooms where they will sleep, the bathrooms, and especially the showers. They peer out the windows and into the closets and at the participants whom they do not yet know. Olympic Village is a hive of activity, and voices babble with excitement.

Dinnertime arrives. Sometimes there is a banquet, the dining hall bright with the Special Olympics blue and gold. The participants sit at long tables, beside old friends and friends to be. Names and addresses are written on napkins and tucked into small pockets. Sometimes the napkins are taken anyway, as tangible evidence of a dream that is really happening.

After dinner there is entertainment—a mixer with a live band, dancing and punch, or a magician who does mystifying tricks, or a movie. There is a certain shyness among some of the participants as they meet others from across the state and exchange experiences and hopes. Bedtime comes all too soon, although it is exciting to troop to the showers with new friends, to crawl between the sheets of a bed one has never slept in before, and to listen to the sounds, as all over Olympic Village participants prepare to retire for the night.

Morning comes, and Olympic Village bustles with activity. In their rooms, the participants don the uniforms, special caps or outfits that will distinguish their group from those representing other towns or counties or schools. Breakfast is welcomed, for in the excitement of the previous evening not many ate a full dinner.

Then they walk, or are bused, to the stadium or field. It is huge to them, and filled with activity. Here and there, bands practice their marching tunes. Coaches, chaperons, and guides hurry about. There is an air of excited anticipation as the groups and bands take their places for the opening parade. Then the starting whistle, and the drums begin the marching tempo. Dressed alike and displaying flags and banners to identify their groups, stepping to the familiar drumbeats that mean parade excitement to every American, the participants march proudly past the reviewing stand. Important people are in the stand to greet them—members of the Kennedy family or people from Special Olympics, Inc., mayors, the governor, sports and show-business personalities. The parade continues around the field and finally comes to a halt, the groups situated so that all can see the bright flags and the crowds in the stands and what happens next. The American flag is raised while the national anthem is played. Then, a hush falls upon the crowd. Far down the track a proud young runner becomes visible. He carries the Special Olympics torch, and as he draws nearer the only sound that can be heard is the flapping of the multicolored flags. The Flame of Hope is lit, the gold-and-blue Special Olympics flag is raised. There are short speeches from those on the reviewing stand and then the entire assemblage joins in reciting the Special Olympics oath: *"Let me win, but if I cannot win, let me be brave in the attempt."* For a moment there is silence as spectators and participants ponder the meaning of those words. This is not a time just for winners but for anyone who is willing to try. Then, suddenly, thousands of helium-filled balloons are released, and they mingle in the air with the cheers of the crowd.

Now the events begin, and there is action all over. In the field, track and field events like running and high jumping and softball throwing; inside, swimming and bowling and basketball. The surroundings are strange—it's not at all like the playground or pool back home—but the entrants are confident. They have been training and practicing so hard for this moment. They are familiar with the gun that begins the races, the track or pool or bowling lane is the same length as back home. They have been prepared, they know what to do, and they give the effort all they have.

No matter how each participant performs, the effort is rewarded. At the finish line "huggers" await every competitor to congratulate and praise him whether he is first or last. Immediately after each event, the winners are escorted to the awards area and the tiered winners platform. The first, second, and third place winners mount the tiers and are presented their medals. They hear the time in which they ran the race, or the distance they

9. Ethel Kennedy congratulates a winner from Indiana at the International Special Olympics Games.

10. At the starting gun, youngsters plunge into the swimming competition at the 1974 Indiana State Games.

11. Special Olympics has proved that the retarded can develop athletic skills and abilities far beyond those of which they were formerly thought capable.

12. Months of training are behind the grace of her stride and the determination in her face as this young athlete runs in a track event in New Jersey Special Olympics competition.

13. A young gymnast, poised on the balance beam, during the 1975 International Special Olympics Games, Mt. Pleasant, Michigan.

14. One of the participants in the Girl's Softball Throw at the International Special Olympics Games, 1975.

15. With a final, winning leap, a young athlete breaks the tape in indoor-track competition at the North Dakota Special Olympics Games.

16. These little ones try so hard, and whether they finish first or last they are rewarded with love and encouragement.

17. "I won! I won! I won!"

18. The support of personalities in the entertainment field, like Sally Struthers, star of television's "All in the Family," has been important to the growth of the Special Olympics. Their appearances help generate publicity, and help make the young athletes feel very special.

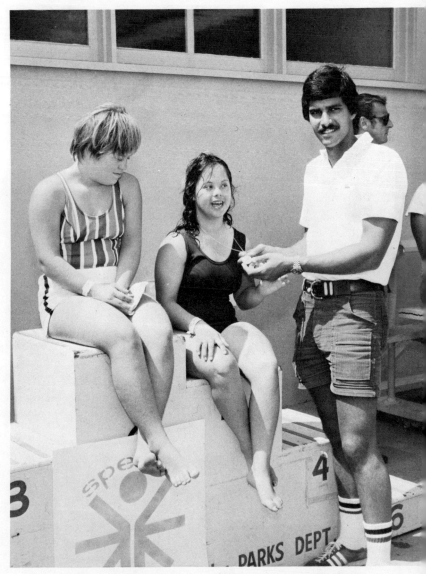

19. Being presented their winning medals by celebrities in the athletic field means much to young athletes. Here, Olympic gold medal swimming champion Mark Spitz is shown with Special Olympics medal winners in swimming competition.

threw the ball, and they know they have done well. A photographer takes their pictures; their families and coaches applaud, and no matter what is happening elsewhere on the field, this is their moment; this is their victory.

In the softball throw area, a little boy beams as he clutches his bronze medal. Over there, a girl who has won the 50-yard dash jumps up and down in excitement. At the swimming pool, the parents of three winners want their pictures taken with their children as the youngsters proudly stand on the platform, their medals on ribbons around their necks.

In between events, the participants enjoy a variety of clinics—physical fitness, the trampoline, basketball, many others. Often, these clinics are conducted by well-known sports personalities. The participants watch and listen and learn new skills in an atmosphere so exciting they hardly realize that they are learning.

The events and clinics take place from midmorning to late afternoon, but no one goes hungry. Box lunches are provided for each group at a designated time and place on the field. The food is the best they have ever tasted—like hot dogs at a baseball game or cotton candy at the circus.

The events continue; the participants press on. For those who have completed their individual competition for the day, there are more clinics and group activities like relay races.

Late in the afternoon, the Olympic Village, familiar now, welcomes the returning competitors. Some sport medals, gleaming gold, silver, and bronze. Others, ribbons and patches. All feel a sense of victory. All want to share this feeling with their friends, old and new.

After dinner, often a victory banquet, there is more fun. Medals on bright-colored ribbons adorn long dresses and suits at the dance or mixer. There is no shyness now, for the differences of age and locality have been overshadowed by the shared experience of competing and belonging.

Bedtime preparations are quieter that evening, as participants savor that last walk down to the showers, that last click of the light switch, that last time of listening to the sounds of Olympic Village as other tired competitors succumb to sleep after a long and exciting day.

In the morning, there are more events and clinics. Participants who have won the previous day win again. Others win for the first time. Still others receive participant ribbons that are just as dear to them as medals. The level of excitement is undiminished. In fact, it increases, for the participants know this is the final day.

At last, all the events are over. The groups from towns and counties across the state muster once more for the final parade, more informal this time, for the participants know each other and call to each other across the lines. They parade onto the field, laughing, talking, pleased with their performances. But all is quiet as the Flame of Hope is extinguished and the torch-bearing runner leaves the field. The flags are lowered, and the participants look across the expanse at the new-found friends whom they must now leave. Slowly, they come together and lock arms, and the dignitaries from the reviewing stand, and the parents and coaches and chaperons join the circle. Together, all assembled sing "Auld Lang Syne."

Many will meet again, at future games or through letters; but whether or not they do meet again they will always have the shared memory of participating, of winning, of competing together. And each will have the memory of a time that was completely and solely theirs.

To an outside observer, the games are so well run that it is hard to imagine the amount of time and effort involved in such a meet. Yet, behind every aspect of the games, from training the participants to financing their trip to the games site, to the closing ceremonies, lies months of work and planning on the part of a veritable army of dedicated and committed volunteers.

Ideally, for months prior to the games, volunteers have been helping the competitors train for the events. In some areas, these volunteers assist coaches or physical education teachers in established physical education programs. In other towns, the training program is entirely run by volunteers. Here, high school students work with children on a one-to-one basis two or three times a week. There, the training of Special Olympians is the special community project of the Jaycees or the Kiwanis Club.

Meanwhile, other volunteers are busy on projects to raise the necessary funds for special uniforms for the participants to wear at the games and to pay the transportation and housing costs for each child. The Kennedy Foundation and Special Olympics, Inc., offer financial assistance in varying degrees on all levels of the Special Olympics program, but state and local committees are encouraged to finance their own programs to the fullest extent possible. Fund-raising projects are an excellent way to acquaint and involve more people in the Special Olympics program and with the needs of the retarded.

There is no end to the range of fund-raising activities in which Special Olympics volunteers engage. Of course, major sources of funds are local businesses and clubs and individual donations. But small sums add up quickly, too. One group ran a "Walk-a-thon" in which a number of high school and college students asked local businessmen to pay a dollar a mile for each mile they walked. Other groups ask well-known entertainers to make benefit appearances. In California, annual "car bashes" are held at which people pay a fee for the privilege of smashing old cars with sledge hammers. In Traverse City, Michigan, in 1974, money to send Cheryl DeLoy and seven other students from her school to area and state games was raised by her classmates, who baked and sold ten thousand doughnuts. Rummage sales, bake sales, raffles, auctions, car washes, sports events—the list of fund-raising activities is as long as the imagination can stretch, and all are conducted by dedicated volunteers.

The Special Olympics Games themselves represent the culmination of months of planning and hard work on the part of volunteers. The logistics involved in housing and feeding all the participants, chaperons, and coaches, not to mention organizing events, awards, and ceremonies are hard to conceive.

Personnel required for a state meet include a meet director, an announcer, a clerk of the course, whose responsibility it is to see that events run off continuously; an event team for each event to see that it is run properly and to record the time, distance, or score for each competitor; runners or escorts to show medal winners to the awards area and present the result sheet to the official recorder; "huggers" to greet each participant as he finishes his event, no matter where he has placed, and congratulate him for his effort; doctors and nurses and other helpers to man the medical units; ambulance and bus drivers; cooks and sandwich makers; sports-clinic directors and workers; and many, many more.

Facilities for feeding and housing all participants are needed. At the 1968 Special Olympics in Chicago, Olympic Village was a hotel. Sometimes an entire residential area becomes an Olympic Village. On the level of state games, colleges and universities are often the host institutions, for they have the dormitory space, the cafeteria facilities, and the athletic areas necessary to accommodate the large numbers of competitors. Another choice site for state games is the military base, for what comparable institution, if willing, is more conversant with the logistical problems involved in accommodating such large numbers of people in such a complex of activities? In Washington State, Fort Lewis Army Base hosted the State Special Olympics for two years in a row. Not only does it have the facilities to accommodate the games and the participants in those games, but also a number of the military personnel who live with their families at Fort Lewis have retarded children. Between Fort Lewis and McCord Air Force Base, there are a sufficient number of handicapped children to populate a special school, American Lake South School. The school's physical education activities are geared toward Special Olympics, and students at the school participate in area and state games.

In 1973, then State Special Olympics Director, Ernest Hoff, approached the commanders of Fort Lewis with the idea of hosting the State Games. While the Post had summer commitments to the ROTC program, it was decided that the Special Olympics could be fit in. The bowling events were held in May and the other events in June. Both meets were successful and particularly well organized, and the following January the Washington Special Olympics Committee asked the Fort to host the games a second year, this time on a single weekend in June.

Lieutenant Colonel Paul Mernaugh, cochairman of the 1974 Washington State Games Committee recalls, "Our unit's involvement with the Special Olympics began in 1973, though we had only a small part of the action. We were in charge of one of the sections with mess halls and billets. The people at Fort Lewis found it a rather large undertaking, so a major-type unit with a lot of men in it was really required to do it. Ours was such a unit, and when we heard that the Fort was going to host the State Games once again, we volunteered to do it.

"Our unit was notified on the first of February that we had been accepted as the host," Mernaugh continues, "and that's when I started work. So much planning and effort goes into the two-day meet that you have to start on it as far ahead as possible. I broke down my responsibilities into sixteen areas because there are so many details. The three largest of these areas, of course, are the games themselves, the Olympic Village, and Special Services."

The various events in the games take place simultaneously, bowling events occurring at the same time as swimming events, running events at the same time as softball throwing, and so on. While both military and civilian volunteers were involved in directing and overseeing these events at Fort Lewis in 1974, civilian volunteers were most highly utilized in this area.

"The State Committee has its group of volunteers," says Lieutenant Colonel Mernaugh, "and in 1974 the Boeing Management Association wanted to help. They sent in the neighborhood of six hundred volunteers to assist in the games area. Primarily military personnel served as bus drivers and guides and things of this nature as well as supervising some of the leisure-time activities. We had strictly military volunteers in the barracks and mess halls."

The late Avery Brundage's LaSalle Hotel was able to accommodate the one thousand participants who competed in the Special Olympics in Chicago in 1968. But many State Games now involve two to three thousand participants, and the barracks of a military base or the dormitories of a large university are best equipped to house such numbers.

"We were flexible," says Lieutenant Colonel Mernaugh. "We set up our billets, or buildings, for forty, and we had forty-eight billets, so we could accommodate somewhere in the neighborhood of two thousand. We also made arrangements so we could put more bunks in the billets if we needed to. So we figured we could house anywhere from two thousand to twenty-four hundred participants and chaperons.

"We made arrangements to have a CQ, a charge of quarters, in each billet to handle whatever problems might come up and be of general assistance. In other words, there might be a problem with one of the bathrooms, or a child has to go upstairs in the middle of the day, and a CQ can help with these things. In 1973 it was found that many of the children could not distinguish among the buildings, which all look the same, and would get into the wrong building. The CQ can help the child find the right one, find out where he belongs."

Feeding all the participants is also a major undertaking. In many states, much of this responsibility is assumed by large restaurants or food or soft drink companies. In some areas, women's clubs take on the task of providing lunch for the participants, preparing in assembly-line fashion four thousand sandwiches of various kinds and baking far into the night so that each participant will have cookies for dessert. Hot meals for that many people can best be provided by facilities such as university dining halls or military mess halls.

"Fort Lewis," says Mernaugh, "has twelve mess halls, or eating facilities, and we manned each with a cook, a mess steward, and KPs, all working on a volunteer basis. Each facility can accommodate anywhere from one hundred twenty to two hundred people, which enabled us to have one scheduled breakfasttime and one scheduled dinnertime. As at lunchtime the participants would be engaging in events, we arranged that sack or box lunches be prepared and delivered to the participants wherever they happened to be. Of course this was also organized, by means of a code system so that if, for example, a youngster was participating in girls' swimming events between noon and 1 P.M., she might eat before or after, depending on the code."

Special Services involves such things as doctors, hospitals, ambulances, transportation, and hospitality of one sort or another. Of course, the major concern is with the health of the participants, many of whom are on medication, and with the possibility of injury, although chances of serious injury are remote.

The *Guide for Local Programs* issued by the Kennedy Foundation makes suggestions in this area to cover all exigencies. Because most of the activity takes place on an open field, shaded areas ought to be provided, water should be available at various sites around the field and should be supervised so that no competitor drinks more than is good for him. Some kind of sunscreening solution should be provided for all participants so that they will not get too sunburned. A main medical station should be set up, but roving medical and first-aid teams ought to be available as well. Obtaining medical personnel is rarely a problem. Individual doctors and hospital staff members are willing volunteers. Ambulances and drivers are provided by hospitals or by local organizations such as the Lions Club. At Fort Lewis, medical personnel are readily available.

"The Post has its own medics," says Lieutenant Colonel Mernaugh, "and four ambulances. The regular civilian hospitals are on call, and each of the participants has his or her own doctor on call. Also, all the participants bring their own medical records in case they are needed. All these things must be organized into an efficient net-work."

Naturally, substantial cost is involved in all the preparations and the actual realization of a two-day state meet. But a hosting institution is not expected to shoulder the burden. The State Special Olympics Committee seeks funds for the state games, and the purpose of many of the major fund-raising activities is to finance the annual state meet.

"There are some expendable supplies that are used in preparation, like cleaning supplies, for which the Post does not expect to be reimbursed," says Lieutenant Colonel Mernaugh. "Other costs, such as for food, have to be refunded. The Special Olympics Committee pretty well picks up the tab. Basically, there is not a great deal of cost for the Post, except for the volunteer labor. That, we cannot put a price tag on."

Volunteers in any worthwhile program receive their own kind of reimbursement. "When it was announced that our unit would host the games in 1974," Mernaugh says, "we received many calls from people who said, 'I helped last year, what can I do to help this year?' It gives one a good feeling to go around and visit and talk to the participants, to watch them and know that whether they finish first, or in the middle, or last, they're still winners. They're as happy with that participation ribbon as they are with a gold medal, and it's great to feel that you've had something to do with that happiness."

Volunteer workers also learn much from their experience, and many are pleased to have had the opportunity to improve their organizational skills. Students at universities that have hosted state games consider working at the games an additional and unexpected part of their education. Even military personnel, for whom precise organization is part of everyday life, benefit.

As Lieutenant Colonel Mernaugh puts it, "It is like a great planning exercise. Of course, the problems are a little different from field problems, but it is a good exercise to solve them. Our transportation people had to lay out bus routes and plan for both scheduled runs and shuttle-type service. We had our food service people working with the State Committee, determining the population to be fed, planning menus, arranging for the box lunches. Our billeting people had to make the buildings ready and determine who should be billeted where. Our medics helped set up a functioning health-care network. So really all this is beneficial experience for a military unit."

In Washington, Special Olympics has benefited in many ways from association with Fort Lewis. Not only has it been able to use the Post's facilities, but also the participants enjoy spending two days at an Army base.

Lieutenant Colonel Mernaugh recalls, "At our initial meeting with the Washington Special Olympics people in 1974, one of their requests was that the military volunteers wear their uniforms. They found out in 1973 that the participants were very impressed with the Army uniform and really enjoyed talking to the soldiers, whom they could distinguish easily. They also enjoy our static display—three different types of helicopters, a tank, and various types of howitzers. The participants can sit in the helicopter and on the tank and move various parts of the equipment."

There is a further benefit from holding the Special Olympics Games on a U.S. military base. The retarded children of American taxpayers are given the opportunity to utilize the base's facilities. And all that expensive war material, when retarded youngsters touch it and climb upon it and sit in it, has a peaceful use.

Is all the work worth it? The answer from the hundreds of thousands of volunteers is an unequivocal and resounding "Yes!" Commenting on the 1972 International Games in a letter to the Kennedy Foundation, Bob Cruce of the Rolla Regional Diagnostic Clinic in Rolla, Missouri, put it this way:

> "For the first time in my life I saw thousands of people that were gathered together because they really cared, not just because it was a job. We sometimes refer to the kids as 'God's perfect children,' and after giving it some thought, it is these same children that we work with that mold our lives into more perfect adults."

Chapter V: The 1975 International Special Olympics Games

On August 7–11, 1975, the fourth International Special Olympics was held at Central Michigan University in Mt. Pleasant, Michigan. The site was chosen because of CMU's excellent athletic facilities and strong program in special education. The school also had a rich tradition in volunteer programs, and one of the most important bases of the Special Olympics program is its corps of dedicated volunteers.

It took more than a year of planning and work on the part of Central Michigan University and the Michigan Special Olympics Committee, assisted by Special Olympics, Inc., to produce the largest and most successful International Games to date, but when it was all over, ev-

eryone agreed that they had been more than rewarded for
their efforts. None were more pleased than the participants themselves, for they had worked and practiced and
competed long months in order to go to the Internationals.

Ranging in age from ten to seventy, they came from
every state of the Union, plus the District of Columbia,
and many foreign countries: Belgium, Brazil, Canada,
France, West Germany, Mexico, the Philippines, and El
Salvador. Three thousand two hundred strong, they
represented some 400,000 participants in the year-round
Special Olympics program and had qualified by competing in over 15,000 local and state meets. It was an honor
for each one of them to be coming to the games, and from
the moment they arrived they knew just how special they
were.

At Capitol City Airport, in Lansing, where the planes
landed with Special Olympians en route to Central Michigan University, a red carpet was rolled out on the run-
way, and the various state delegations were delighted
with the loudspeaker greeting they received from city
emergency operations director, Bob Holcomb. "Let's hear
it for the delegation from New Jersey! Best of luck to you!
You look like number one," Holcomb would bellow as the
New Jersey Special Olympians walked or were carried
down the steps of the DC-8 jet. Holcomb had spent days
gathering records of as many state "fight songs" as he
could find, and when the Texas delegation arrived the
participants cheered happily as Holcomb played "The
Eyes of Texas Are Upon You." Well-wishers who had
come to watch the arrival of the Special Olympians

cheered each delegation; photographers' flash bulbs lit up the sky. "Cheese!" smiled a twenty-one-year-old girl from New Jersey as, after a painful, step-by-step descent down the stairs, she plopped triumphantly into her wheelchair.

In the airport parking lot a convoy of buses waited to take the participants and their coaches and chaperons on the last lap of the journey to Mt. Pleasant. Most would stay in the town of Mt. Pleasant itself, which had been turned into an Olympic Village; but there would be so many reporters and photographers and visiting dignitaries that not only spare rooms in private homes would be filled but also every motel room for a twenty-mile radius around Mt. Pleasant.

All Wednesday afternoon and Thursday the delegations continued to arrive. Opening ceremonies were held early Thursday evening so that two full days, Friday and Saturday, could be devoted to the tremendously complex task of seeing that each participant was able to enter at least two individual contests and one relay event in the large number of competitive offerings.

Praise for the Computer Age! With thirty-two hundred participants and the need for over a thousand separate contests, CMU's Univac 1106 computer performed a vital function. Early in July individual entry information was fed into the computer, analyzed, and reproduced in a series of special reports. The reports assigned individuals to specific events on the basis of sex, age, and ability. For example, more than one hundred twenty-five participants were expected to enter the bowling competition. They would compete in separate male and female groupings.

Each grouping by sex was subdivided into age groupings. Then the age groups were further divided into ability groups. Who would have thought, back in 1968 at the first International Games, that a mere seven years later a computer would be needed to assign participants to competition divisions in the bowling events?

The list of events alone says much about the tremendous expansion of the Special Olympics in its brief lifetime. Team sports such as basketball, floor hockey, and volleyball had once been thought too demanding for the mentally retarded. Track and field events have been expanded to include wheelchair events so that retarded people in wheelchairs might also participate. Swimming events now include diving competition. Gymnastic events have been expanded, bowling has been added, and at the 1975 Internationals ice skating was featured for the first time. Many states had held successful Winter Special Olympics, and it was felt that participants from these states should have the opportunity to demonstrate their skills on ice.

Another feature, new to the Internationals, was the corps of volunteer "huggers" whose duty it was to wait at the finish lines to meet each contestant at the end of his or her event and to praise the contestant for doing well. They escorted the contestants to the records table and then to the awards table or back to their groups.

While both local and international meets have always featured warm greetings for each participant, the term "huggers" originated at Central Michigan University during the 1973 State Games. Bruce Saltman of Flint, Michigan, thought of giving each participant a hug because he didn't want anyone to feel left out after the events. At the 1975 Internationals volunteers wore green and white badges proclaiming "I Am a Hugger," and they included student volunteers from CMU as well as such celebrities as actresses Susan Saint James and Sally Struthers.

Many other celebrities and celebrity athletes volunteered in various capacities at the 1975 Internationals, and from the time CMU was chosen to host the games until the time the last delegation departed, some one thousand volunteers had worked on the International Games alone, not to mention some 150,000 others who worked on the state, area, and local level in other states and countries training Special Olympians and raising money for their programs.

No one knows better than Eunice Kennedy Shriver how much Special Olympics depends for its existence upon volunteers. "Without volunteer support," she says, "without willing hands and caring hearts—the mentally retarded would not be able to take part in those activities we have historically reserved for the 'normal.'" Volunteers can be found on all levels of the Special Olympics program. Seventy-five per cent of the state Special Olympics directors are volunteers, and those few who are paid understand fully that they could do little without volunteer help. As for the volunteer "huggers" and sports clinic operators, the sandwich makers and bus drivers, the fund raisers and escorts, and all the other volunteers in all their other capacities, they do not get medals or any particular recognition. What they do get is the warm and happy feeling that they are doing something very special, interacting with people who are hungry for attention and affection.

Each year, more and more Special Olympians show how very much they deserve this attention and affection, and the participants at the 1975 International Special Olympics were no exception. One of the newest and most moving Special Olympics success stories is that of Mike Baker, who was born not just retarded but also with only one leg. A black foster child, Mike's double handicap kept him out of many activities for most of his fourteen years. In the spring of 1975, Charles Miller, coach at the Southwest Training Center near Detroit, decided to get Mike involved in the Special Olympics program. Mike trained in gymnastics both at school and at home, practicing his tumbling on mats and performing on a home-made balance beam. With each hour of practice, his skill and confidence increased, and when time for the area Special Olympics came, he convinced Miller to let him enter the 220-yard dash as well.

On the day of the games, the 220-yard dash was the first of Mike's events scheduled. He finished dead-last, but he finished, and the loss did not dampen his spirit at all. He went on to win first place on the balance beam and second place in tumbling.

Chosen as one of the one hundred Special Olympians from Wayne County, Michigan, to compete in the 1975 International Games, Mike told his coach that he was going to win first place not only on the balance beam but also in tumbling. Arriving at Central Michigan University, both were disappointed that no balance beam event had been included in the International Games. But after his initial disappointment, Mike became more determined than ever to win in tumbling. He did, and he beamed as the gold medal was placed around his neck. He held it lightly with both hands, his fingers barely touching it, as if his holding it too tightly might cause it to disappear.

Next came the Michigan State Special Olympics Games. Once more, Mike won a gold medal on the balance beam and a silver medal in tumbling. He won something else as well. The youngster who had once finished last was named the games' "Most Inspirational Athlete."

Mike Baker was fourteen when he went to the 1975 International Games; Corrine Scruggs was seventy. Mentally handicapped and confined to a wheelchair, she took her first airplane ride traveling from Florida to participate in the games at Central Michigan University. There, she entered the 25-yard wheelchair run and the softball throw, wearing her red "good luck" baseball cap. After competing, she was asked if she wanted to take a nap or go to a baseball game. Her answer was unequivocal.

"Play ball," she said.

At CMU she enjoyed rolling her wheelchair over the winding campus paths and watching the younger participants compete. But, she said, she was glad she could have her fun, too.

The love Special Olympians show for each other can be a lesson to all of us. No matter how intent they are on competing in their own events, they find time to encourage or console others, some of whom they have never met before. In one relay, a little girl from Colorado fell and started to cry. A big hand reached out to her and helped her up. The male athlete from Alabama smiled down at her and said, "It's all right. You'll get another chance and I'll bet you'll win." The two walked off the track hand in hand, and both were smiling.

Ron Requilman, twenty-one, one of the sixty-five participants from the District of Columbia, held his gold medal for the mile run and his eyes filled with tears. "We're all in this together, black and white, big and small, and young and old," he said. "We're brothers and sisters and maybe we do have a handicap. But we can compete in anything we want to. All we ask was for a chance."

It was the first day of competition at the 1975 International Games, and already Requilman, who is white, and three of his black teammates had each won a gold medal. All but one were wearing their medals. Laurence Robinson, twenty-one, who had won his in the softball throw, had given it to his coach for safekeeping. The four were sitting on a bench, resting, when a thirteen-year-old girl came up to Robinson and asked if he was going to watch her run her track events the next day.

"Sure thing. We'll all be there cheering you on. And if you don't win a gold medal," said the young athlete who prized his own medal so much that he had entrusted it to his coach, "I'll give you mine."

That's what Special Olympics encourages—not winning or losing but trying and sharing. Special Olympics has enjoyed remarkable growth since its inception, and while there are still many more mentally retarded people to be reached, there are strong indications that eventually they will be, for Special Olympics is an idea whose time has come.

Media coverage of the 1975 International Special Olympics Games far exceeded that of any previous International Games. Not only were the games the subject of over seven thousand newspaper and magazine articles here and abroad but also, for the first time, they were featured as an entire segment of "CBS Sports Spectacular," receiving equal coverage with a number of other major national sporting events. Almost everywhere, there is an increasing awareness that the mentally handicapped are capable of engaging in, and benefiting from, regular physical activity and athletic competition. The philosophy that participation and good sportsmanship outweigh considerations of winning and losing is making itself felt.

It can be seen in the attitude of seventeen-year-old Bob Hamon of Colorado Springs, Colorado. Hamon, who is deaf and mute, had traveled twelve hundred miles to participate in the high jump competition at the 1975 International Special Olympics. As he prepared to make his jump, he could not hear the din of the crowd in the stands. His entire concentration on the high metal bar, he accelerated and leaped skyward. Clang! The metal bar dropped to the asphalt below. A groan went up from the crowd. Bob Hamon did not hear either sound. But he had felt the bar give under his weight, and he realized he had failed. The look on his face showed the anguish he could not express in words.

But the look was only momentary, for immediately he was surrounded by his coaches and friends. They hugged him, and showed him that they were proud he had tried so hard. Then they pointed to the crowd. "Look," they signified. "They are proud of you, too." Bob Hamon could not hear the cheers and applause, but he could see the crowd. The spectators were standing; their mouths were smiling, voicing soundless encouragement; their hands clapped in a vacuum of silence. And now another emotion welled up inside Bob Hamon. With tear-filled eyes he scanned the packed bleachers and then he began to smile.

Chapter VI: Some Very Special Olympians

JERRY JOE GORRELL

Putnam County, Indiana, is a very rural area, practically devoid of industry, dependent for its livelihood on truck farming. People must work hard there to make ends meet, and their aspirations are simple—a comfortable home, enough food to eat, a peaceful family life, and an occasional night out at the town movie theater or at the church social. The tensions and concern with social position that afflict the cities are not found here, and there is little stigma attached to retardation.

Still, there is a definite awareness that the retarded do require special help, and this awareness is due in large measure to the manner in which the state of Indiana deals with its handicapped population. Not every town in Indiana, of course, cares equally about its retarded youngsters and the programs that are developed to help them. And not all parents of a retarded child are firmly committed to their child's realization of his fullest potential. Jerry Joe Gorrell has been fortunate in having both.

Jerry Joe Gorrell was born in Putnam County on March 14, 1955, the first child of Charles and Imogene Gorrell. Four years later, Robert was born, and two years after that Kenneth arrived. By the time Kenneth was born, Jerry had been diagnosed as retarded, and Mrs. Gorrell had determined to do everything possible to see that her son developed to the best of his ability.

"I have been with Special Education ever since Jerry started school," she said in 1974. "I don't know as they have official room mothers in Special Education classes, but I guess I have been unofficial room mother for every one of Jerry's classes up until this year."

In Indiana, each school district, if possible, is expected to provide special classes for its retarded youngsters. "But," says Sharon McCammon, Jerry's former teacher, "a lot of the counties are thinly populated, perhaps twenty-five to thirty-five thousand people, and there are not enough children in any one school district to make special classes feasible for that district. Putnam County has four or five school districts, but none has a sufficient number of retarded kids to make up classes geared to different age groups or intelligence levels. So the districts co-operate and have county classes to which the kids are,

20. The emblem on his tee shirt expressing an important goal of Special Olympics, a young athlete clears the eight-foot bar with infinite finesse. Rafer Johnson, an early and energetic supporter of Special Olympics, urges the young man on.

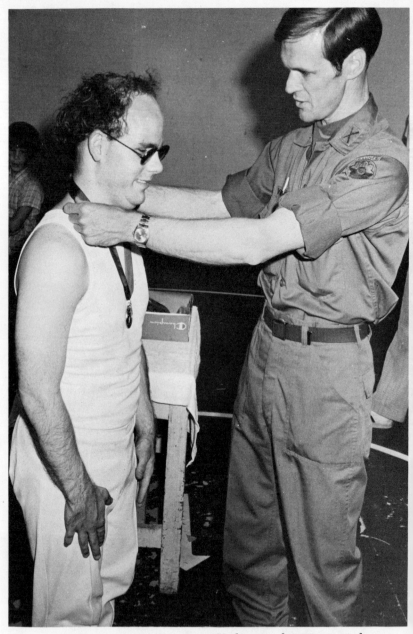

21. Eric Swanson of Tacoma, Washington, being presented with a gold medal for gymnastics in the 1973 Washington Special Olympics. Though both retarded and blind, Eric is nationally recognized for his gymnastic ability.

22. The spotlight his own, Stevie Waddell beams with pleasure at having completed the twenty-five-yard swim in the 1974 Florida Special Olympics Games. Mrs. Rose Kennedy presents official congratulations.

23. Karl Wiedel, sporting the medals he won in the 1974 Maryland Special Olympics Games, applauds the performance of a fellow competitor.

24. This young winner can hardly contain his excitement as State Senator Esther Sorrell presents his medal to him at the 1974 Vermont State Games.

25. Eunice Kennedy Shriver presents medals to Special Olympics winners in Michigan.

26. Ann Prothero, proud medal winner in International Special Olympics swimming competition.

27. Two young Crow Indians proudly display their first- and second-place medals at Montana State Games.

28. This is what Special Olympics is all about, and the young athletes recognize it.

29 & 30. One of the nicest things about Special Olympics is sharing your happiness with your friends.

ideally, bused in." The Gorrells lived in an area that participated in such co-operative special education.

"When Jerry first started school," says Mrs. Gorrell, "I was driving eighty-four miles a day with him, to get him to class in Greencastle and back; and I did that for three or four years. We needed a Special Education teacher in the North Putnam school district then, and another lady and I worked until we got a teacher up in that area, who is still there."

Once a Special Education teacher had been sent to the North Putnam school district, Jerry was able to go to school closer to home, and he attended school in the area until he was sixteen. At that time, the Gorrells moved to Roachdale, a small community in Putnam County, and Jerry enrolled in North Putnam Jr.-Sr. High School, a special school.

Jerry grew into a serious, responsible young man, well-behaved both at home and at school.

"This boy is nineteen years old," said Mrs. Gorrell in 1974, "and I can sit here and honestly say he has never given me a cross word in his life. And that's something you can't say about most nineteen-year-old boys these days."

"He is a very good-natured kid," said Sharon McCammon, Jerry's teacher at Greencastle High School, in 1974, "and he's well-behaved. He relates well with everyone in the class, but he doesn't especially hang around with those boys who like to get into mischief. At the end of the year, it was getting hot and everyone was ready for school to end two weeks before it did, just as in every class—even Jerry and one other girl in the class who are especially nice, nice people. And I knew it had to be the end of the year, because even Jerry was talking out in class.

"There aren't many social activities for the students in a rural area like that. The university nearby has a youth association for retarded children, and the college students who are interested in helping out sponsor dances for the kids. I attended two of them, and brought the students in my class who wanted to go and didn't have a way. Jerry went both times.

"The dances were held in the basement of a fraternity house, and the guys and girls from the college would dance with the kids, which would thrill them. One of the times, a little girl in my class who wears arm crutches had invited a little boy to come, and he had not come. In fact, he had sent someone else in his place. So she just sat and cried, she was so upset. On the first dance, Jerry went over and asked her to be his partner, and from then on everything was all right. After Jerry asked her to dance, the other guys did, too. Jerry is very sensitive to other people's feelings."

Ever since Jerry entered school, Mrs. Gorrell says, she maintained a careful watch over his education and kept abreast of new opportunities for retarded youngsters. In 1969, when the first Special Olympics Games were held in Indiana, Mrs. Gorrell heard of the event from Jerry's teacher and decided that Jerry should participate.

Both she and her husband were impressed with the warmth of the people at Indianapolis and with their efforts to encourage reluctant parents to join in the spirit of the games. "There is nothing to be ashamed of," says Mrs. Gorrell.

"Nobody makes fun of anyone at the events," Mr. Gorrell adds, "and we've been to so many."

"We started in with the '69 Olympics," Mrs. Gorrell said in 1974, "and we've been to every one since. Part of the time we had teachers to help us, and part of the time we didn't; we just came on our own."

While every student at North Putnam Jr.-Sr. High School received regular physical education instruction, the school's physical education program was not particularly geared toward the Special Olympics. It was Mrs. Gorrell who saw that her son went to the 1972 state games at Indiana State University at Terre Haute.

"That was the year we brought him down here all by ourselves," says Mrs. Gorrell. "We had no teacher and no coach—we just brought him.

"I guess you could say we organized that community," she continues. "I just felt that some kids from there should go to Terre Haute, and we would pick them up and take them here and pay the bills."

At Terre Haute, Jerry entered two track and field events as well as a swimming event. Swimming against others in the sixteen- to eighteen-year-old bracket, Jerry won his heat and then placed third in the finals. Dr. Thomas Songster, cochairman of the Indiana Special Olympics at that time, was also coach of the swimming team that would go to the International Games in Los Angeles. He saw Jerry's potential, and Mrs. Gorrell could not have agreed with him more.

"You ought to have seen my wife the day they said he was going to California," says Mr. Gorrell. "She didn't even ask Jerry if he wanted to go."

One of the most striking aspects of Jerry Gorrell's story is the manner in which the community of Roachdale, to which the Gorrells were fairly new, rallied to his support.

"We went back home," Mrs. Gorrell says, "and I have a friend who is in a sorority there, and she got busy and I got busy, and the money started rolling in. It was going to cost three hundred and some odd dollars to get Jerry out to California, and in no time flat the money was there."

Meanwhile, the time of the International Special Olympics approached, and Jerry, a quiet, unassuming young man, was suddenly struck by the reality of the event about which everyone around him was so excited. He, Jerry Gorrell, who had been born and brought up in rural Putnam County, and whose longest previous journeys had been to Indianapolis and Terre Haute, was going to California, on a plane! He wasn't at all sure that he wanted to go, but his mother seemed so excited and he did not want to disappoint her. He said nothing.

Sometimes, parents express misgivings about sending their retarded children to the Special Olympics Games, for they are afraid the children will not react well to a strange environment far away from home. In the case of the Gorrells, it was the youngster who had misgivings.

"I pushed him all the way," Mrs. Gorrell admits, "and you know, the evening we took him over to the Holiday Inn in Indianapolis, I got to thinking . . . I never did ask him if he wanted to go . . . and then he was gone.

"I felt really badly about it. If anything had happened to him . . . But it had just never entered my mind to ask him whether he wanted to go or not.

"We left him at the Holiday Inn at about three-thirty in the afternoon," Mrs. Gorrell continues, "and that night we were sitting at home watching television when the phone rang and it was Jerry."

Mrs. Gorrell continues, "I said 'What's the matter, Jerry, are you sick?' and he said, 'Well, I think I'm getting that way.'"

"Homesick," Jerry now reveals.

"So I told him he'd be all right and we'd be up there the next morning," says Mrs. Gorrell. "When we got there, they were all eating breakfast, and his face was all swollen and tears were in his eyes. He was really upset.

"So I took him out and talked to him, and got him settled down; and when he got on the plane he was having as much fun as the rest. He called me on Sunday, as soon as he got there and said they had made it all right and everything was fine."

Jerry does not talk very much, but he is proud to be able to say that he has been on a plane and that he has traveled to California, considerably farther than most people he knows have traveled. To this Midwesterner, the most striking thing about California was the ocean— "Big." He enjoyed staying in the UCLA dormitory, but Mrs. Gorrell questions whether he enjoyed the food.

"He likes everything except eggs," she says. "When he was in California, they fed him eggs all the time I think, and he's hardly eaten an egg since he came home."

Seventy youngsters from Indiana represented their state at UCLA in 1972. Among them was Ann Prothero, mentioned earlier in Chapter IV, from Terre Haute. The two formed a close relationship while in California and have kept in touch ever since by means of telephone calls and letters. While Jerry says that he has *two* girlfriends, he admits that his favorite is Ann.

The 1972 International Special Olympics events in which Jerry Gorrell participated took place on a Tuesday and Wednesday.

Mrs. Gorrell recalls, "Tuesday night he called me, and he said, 'Mother, I'm warning you . . .' and I knew he had won. He won first place in two events and he was going to be in a play-off the next day.

"On Wednesday, he called back, and he said, 'Mother, I've won again. I won a first-place medal and a second-place medal.'"

On Tuesday, Jerry had participated in the heats for the 25-yard and 50-yard freestyle swimming events, winning first place and a blue ribbon in each heat. On Wednesday, in the finals, he had won a gold medal for the 25-yard event and a silver medal for the 50-yard event.

"Well, I'm telling you," Mrs. Gorrell continues, "that community wasn't big enough for me. There were several people waiting at our house for his call, and they went home and started calling other people. The newspapers wrote about him and everything."

The file of clippings on Jerry Gorrell is probably as thick as that of any other personality in the Roachdale area, if not thicker. There was no question that the town considered him a hero. Upon his return from California, which trip had included not only the International Special Olympics but a visit to Disneyland as well, Jerry spoke before a gathering of the civic organizations that had raised the money to send him to UCLA.

"Our little community up there," says Mrs. Gorrell, "our little town of Roachdale is no bigger than one or two thousand. But they're behind anything like this 100 per cent. And, of course, since Jerry's gone to California they're even more that way. If we were to tell them today that we needed money to send him somewhere else, by tomorrow night they'd have the money raised. And we haven't lived there more than three or four years either. That's just the way they are. And if a little community can do that, so can big ones."

Being a celebrity has not affected Jerry. He is still as quiet and unassuming as he always was. He does not feel he is due special favors.

"He worked in the cafeteria second semester of last year," said Sharon McCammon in 1974, "and the supervisor told me that since Jerry started working fewer things get knocked off and broken and things are done more neatly.

"Also, the Special Olympics are very important to Jerry, but the only time we could practice he had to work. So he would work thirty to forty minutes of the fifty-five-minute period when we swam, and only after he had finished work would he practice his swimming. And he didn't do his work in a haphazard way in order to get into the pool earlier. His job came before his swimming, which is his biggest pleasure in the world. As much as he wanted to go to the Regionals, he would not commit himself to going until after I had spoken to the cafeteria supervisor. Jerry just has an inward sense of responsibility—that if you have a job, your first duty is to that job."

Jerry did go to the 1974 Regional Special Olympics at

Wabash College in Crawfordsville. In fact, he served as Grand Marshal and Special Guest at the games. He also attended the 1974 State Special Olympics at Terre Haute, where he was quite well known among the members of the Indiana Special Olympics Committee and among other seasoned Special Olympians. Quite unlike the frightened, homesick youngster who set out for California in 1972, Jerry was now very much at ease at Special Olympics Games, and when he is at ease his dry wit surfaces.

"One night," says Sharon McCammon, "somebody was whistling outside the dormitory and Jerry called out, 'Did you lose your dog?' He comes up with things like that, and they're not trite, they're his originals."

At the state games, Jerry won three medals, as well as ribbons, in track and field and swimming and had the opportunity to visit with Ann Prothero.

In June, 1975, Jerry Joe Gorrell graduated from Greencastle High School, having fulfilled the graduation requirements for the state of Indiana. After that, Mrs. Gorrell hoped he could continue his schooling. If not, both she and her husband thought he would do well at a job working with machines. He is very good with mechanical things.

"He's my right-hand man," says Mrs. Gorrell proudly. Mr. Gorrell adds, "Anything there is to be fixed, if it can be fixed, he'll fix it, televisions, radios, anything."

"Jerry is the rare kind of person who could be placed just about anywhere," said Sharon McCammon, "and he's so conscientious that he would do a good job. He lives in a very rural area; it's not industrialized and there are no transportation facilities. Unless some transportation arrangements are made for him, Jerry will probably do farm work of some sort. But he really will do all right, I know."

Two months after graduation, in August, Jerry got a job with the Universal Tank and Iron Company at Avon, Indiana, where he would be trained in welding. He no longer participates in Special Olympics, but because of his involvement with the Special Olympics he will always have something that too many retarded youths still do not have the opportunity for. As Mrs. Gorrell puts it, "Always before, these kids had the idea that they were different and they couldn't do anything. The Special Olympics shows they can, and it has given them a place in life."

SUSAN CONN

Susan Conn is an adopted child. In fact, all three children of Charles and Catherine Conn are adopted. Their first was a boy, Steve, and then came Susan who, the Conns thought, was a normal baby. But when Susan was two, she was diagnosed as having brain damage and epilepsy.

"At first it was quite a shock," says Catherine Conn, "to think you have a normal child and then all of a sudden to find that there is something wrong with her—after they have told you that everything's fine. For a while, for perhaps the first year, it was hard; but after that it wasn't. Once we had accepted the idea that she wasn't going to get better, we were able to embrace the philosophy, live for today and let tomorrow take care of itself."

Clearly, the Conns did not just pay lip service to that philosophy. After such an experience as theirs, other couples might have shied away from further involvement with adoption, but the Conns went ahead and adopted a second son, Mark. While suffering from normal sibling rivalry problems among the children, who at this writing were aged seventeen, sixteen, and fourteen, the family has been close. They have always done things together, particularly outdoor things, and Susan's interest in athletics is a natural and longstanding one. Her older brother, Steve, is involved in gymnastics and swimming.

"We are a very athletically inclined family," says Mrs. Conn, "and Susan has always participated with us, joined with us in all of our ventures—backpacking, bicycle trips, etc. She's always been right there, in everything we do. When we go backpacking, she's always at the front of the line. She wants to be the leader. With some of these kids, the only time they get to participate in physical activity is at school. Their families don't do things together as we do."

Susan, a pretty girl with shoulder-length brown hair, has gone to special schools all her life, and she has been fortunate in going to schools where regular physical education is included in the curriculum. It was in 1971 that Susan first became involved in the Special Olympics.

"We had this gym teacher for track and field," says Susan, "and our gym teacher just got us into it."

In her first State Special Olympics Games, Susan won medals in running and in gymnastics, specifically "jumping over the leather horse," as Susan puts it.

"She was so excited and very proud of what she had done," Mrs. Conn recalls. "It was the first time she had ever won anything, all by herself. We were sold on the Special Olympics from that time on."

Susan did not, however, become involved in a program of physical activity geared specifically to the Special Olympics until she entered Lake Washington Special Education School. The director of physical education there was Ernest Hoff, head of Washington State Special Olympics from 1972 to 1974.

"It's been so good for her to be involved in that kind of program," said Mrs. Conn in 1974. "It has given her a real goal to work for. Such a program gives the kids a sense of purpose; it gives them the impetus to train a little more, to practice a little more. Of course Ernie Hoff has a lot to do with it. He's really behind the kids. He instills in them, inspires in them, a desire to do their best—win or lose, to do their best. And he's used the program to teach them a lot of other things. Weight control, proper eating, proper sleep, and exercise—all these little things go along with the program, too.

In 1974, Mrs. Conn pointed out, "he took the time to have an afterschool gym class, an hour every Thursday, so the kids could train more for the Spring Olympics Games. And he introduces new skills. They've been working on the long jump, and more track events."

Under Hoff's tutelage, Susan developed not only her track and field skills but her swimming skills as well. Now, her favorite pastime is swimming. At this writing, she is practicing what she describes as "a swan dive, backwards—a back dive and forward somersault." She hopes to be able to dive from the high board someday, but for now, as she considers diving "scary," she stays on the low board.

Special Olympics, however, has given her the confidence to try nearly anything. In the 1974 State Special Olympics Games, she entered the bowling competition for the first time, after having joined an afterschool bowling program organized by Hoff.

"She really likes bowling," says her older brother, Steve. "They bowl after school, and she comes home from bowling and we sit down to eat, and she has to tell everyone her scores. She really gets excited about it."

Steve Conn also feels that Susan has changed as a result of participating in the Special Olympics program, although in a different way: "She used to fight, but she wasn't that good at it," he says, "but all this practicing has developed her muscular co-ordination, I guess. Now if you get in a fight with her, watch out!"

Susan Conn leads the life of a very normal teen-ager. She fights frequently with her brothers.

"She'll get mad at the boys if they haven't been genial," chuckles Mrs. Conn. "What is her favorite expression? 'I asked them very nicely to do this.'—'I asked them very nicely to do this and do you know what they said?' And then she'll get on her high horse."

Susan experiments, like any other teen-age girl, with things that will change her appearance. Lake Washington School holds various activities to raise funds to send its candidates to the Special Olympics. "Once," Mrs. Conn recalls, "she came from the school Olympics sale with a blond wig that she had bought as a present for me. She wanted to try it on to see if the boys would recognize her. Steve and one of his friends came into the kitchen, and they started laughing because she looked, she really did look like a guinea pig we had. But Susan decided that it was not her face that they had recognized but her shirt. And I thought that was great."

She likes to listen to records, particularly Neil Diamond's. She also spends a great deal of time on the telephone talking to her girlfriends, which is normal for a teen-age girl, although Susan has a more practical reason than most. Being in a special school designed to serve the special education youngsters in a fairly large area, the students do not generally live in the same neighborhood or within easy walking distance. In fact, Susan is a bit lonesome for friends when not in school, and during the summer Mrs. Conn tries to take Susan and her friends on outings so that they can be together.

At the Lake Washington School, Susan takes a variety of subjects geared to her particular needs. "They don't really grade us," says Susan. "We have a cooking classroom, we cook and do arithmetic—not arithmetic but math. We do spelling. We have art, music, and we have shop and gym." Susan says she likes arithmetic best because she likes to work with numbers. In cooking class, she enjoys making dinners, and sometimes she cooks dinner at home.

"But mostly I cook cookies and cakes at home," Susan says, "I cook oatmeal cookies. My brothers like them, but they won't say they like them."

At school, Susan has a boyfriend named Rick. She is pleased that her mother has met Rick and likes him. They play basketball and baseball together and they take walks. The school sits on a hill at the bottom of which is a newly erected sculpture. Susan and Rick like to walk down to the sculpture, but not hand in hand. "Oh no way, no way," laughs Susan.

Rick had participated in the Special Olympics at his former school but so far had not done so at Lake Washington. "I think he's chicken," says Susan. "He says next year he just might do the Olympics." Susan's participation in the Special Olympics undoubtedly has something to do with Rick's change of heart.

Intellectually, Susan has progressed quite well, according to her mother: "In some areas she's a little sharper, in some areas she's a little slower (than other young people her age). She is reading, I think, on the fourth- or fifth-grade level now," Mrs. Conn says.

Susan is aware of her limitations. She loves swimming. In fact, she loves anything connected with water. "I got interested by fish," says Susan. "I like a whole bunch of fish." The Conns used to have a tank filled with fish at home. "But we'd feed them too much, and they'd get fat and die," says Susan. "One thing I want to do, but I don't think I can do it. I want to be an oceanographer . . . but I'd have to go to college first."

Susan's second career choice is: "Airplane stewardess . . . they get to go places." She has been to many places in the area backpacking with her family, and once they traveled to Idaho by car, which, she thinks, is the farthest she's ever been from her home in Kirkland, Washington, about twenty miles from Seattle. If she were an airline stewardess, she would like to go to Hawaii, where she would swim in the clear blue waters that she has seen in travel advertisements on television. But she would like to go to Texas even more than to Hawaii. "It's hot down there, and all the old ghost towns," Susan says. "I think it's neat about the ghost towns because they're very old and they have a little story to all of them."

For the immediate future, however, Susan is interested in achieving what an older friend, Julie West, has been able to accomplish. Julie is one of the original Special Olympians.

"Julie is taking special reading courses at Bellevue College," says Mrs. Conn, "and this is what we hope to get Susan involved in. Julie is working on her General Education Diploma, and she has her driver's license. This is what Susan wants, too. She wants to buy a Volkswagen; she wants to work; she wants to get an apartment with a girlfriend. She has all these goals in life, and more power to her; but she knows she has to take it all one step at a time."

It is, of course, quite possible that Susan would have been pretty much the same Susan even if she had never become involved in the Special Olympics program, but Special Olympics has added another dimension to her life. When asked why she participated in the Special Olympics, she says, "Mostly because it's fun, and I get away from my parents, get away from my brothers, and I get to be with my friends. And because I like working at that stuff [the skills involved in swimming and diving and bowling], working hard for it."

Going into the 1974 Washington Special Olympics Games, Susan had six medals. Asked how she thought she would do in the 1974 games, she answered, "I hope I win. In everything." How would she feel if she lost? She spoke like a true Special Olympian: "I don't really mind, because I know I've been working for it; and that's just the thing about it, just working for it, just doing it, and doing my best."

As a matter of fact, Susan won—a third-place medal in the 25-yard backstroke (time: 25.62 seconds), and a third-place medal in track for the 50-yard dash (time: 8 seconds). She will always have these medals to be proud of, whether she becomes an oceanographer or an airline stewardess or something else. And she will always have the experience of having worked very hard at something—and having succeeded.

JULIE WEST

Julie West is one of the gold medal winners from the first International Special Olympics Games in Chicago in 1968. In fact, she won two gold medals at Chicago, one for swimming and one for track. She is a proud veteran of the Special Olympics program.

Julie's retardation is mild; in fact, it was not discovered until she was six years old.

"Julie is my fourth child," says Ruth West, "and I did not realize right away that there were problems. Granted, I was busy with the other children, and grandparents and such things; but you see, socially she functions all right and her physical co-ordination was all right. We were really not aware that we had serious problems until she started school, and, you know, that first year I thought it was the kindergarten teacher. . . .

"Julie was unable to do the little workbooks that they had for beginning reading and beginning arithmetic, so she repeated kindergarten. When she was not able to function the next year, then we had to get busy with testing, and so forth. This is when we were told that she had brain damage. I believe learning dysfunction is the term they're using now."

"Julie wasn't seriously retarded," says Lawrence West, "and she was also fortunate to have the opportunity to go to good schools and to have a family that cared."

Once her learning dysfunction had been diagnosed, Julie began to attend special schools and, like Susan Conn, she received regular physical education as part of her course of study. "Washington District Special Education Program was very progressive," says Mrs. West.

"As a matter of fact, they were doing things that people said couldn't be done," Mr. West adds.

Swimming was one of the major activities of the program, and it was at school that Julie learned to swim. Mrs. Jean Lehmann, Washington Special Olympics chairperson, was one of Julie's early swimming instructors. Mrs. Lehmann recalls that in the program of beginning swimming skills, Julie could not seem to master the skill of blowing bubbles. As a result, when doing the crawl stroke she held her head out of the water for a very long time. Over the years, however, Julie's skill improved, and when in 1968 it was announced that an International Special Olympics would be held in Chicago, Julie was one of the youngsters chosen to represent the state of Washington.

"Going to Chicago was really a neat thing. Really cool," says Julie.

"After the events there was a big banquet," says Mrs. West, who accompanied her daughter to Chicago. "We were all seated at round tables, and the Kennedy family got up—Robert Kennedy, Jr., and the older boys, Eunice Shriver and Ethel Kennedy were there—and they circulated around the tables. They were dressed in bright colors, so the children could pick them right out, you know, and I just thought they did a terrific job that evening. It was very gracious and warm and loving, and I was very impressed with that. They really do care about the Special Olympics."

"Of course that's one of the reasons why this whole thing has been such a success," says Julie, "that they've really got someone behind it, you know, backing it up, and with the power."

Among Special Olympians and their families there is great respect for the Kennedy family, not only as the moving force behind the Special Olympics but also as people.

"Especially with all the tragedies they've had in the family, you know, really for them to keep on going," Julie adds.

"And that's exactly the infusion that young people need," Mr. West says, "the spirit of getting up and going, because most of these children have led very protected lives."

"Yes," says Mrs. West. "The most important thing

about these games for the young people is that they start
a race and they finish it, even if somebody has to get out
there and help them the rest of the way. They really hus-
tle—even the one in last place is still hustling.

"And that's very important for all these children, because so many times their parents have helped them constantly, picked up after them, not allowed them the
chance to learn to do for themselves. They go to school,
and here again they're helped—you know, little Johnny,
that's hard for you to do, we'll help you."

"I give a lot of the credit to Mr. Hoff," says Julie,
speaking of Ernest Hoff, Washington State Special Olympics director from 1972 to 1974. "You know, he's really the
most great, good guy to have, in school. He gave a lot of
kids confidence. Look at the tumbling program. They said
no way can anybody [retarded] do any tumbling, and
now see how far it's gone."

"People put limitations on these youngsters," Mrs.
West agrees. "I had a teacher tell me once, 'Julie can't
load a dishwasher.' And I looked at the teacher and said,
'Well, she's doing it.' You know, it never occurred to me
that Julie couldn't load a dishwasher."

Julie can do much more than load a dishwasher. In
1970, she had progressed sufficiently to be accepted into a
special program for the handicapped at Bellevue Community College in Bellevue, Washington, stressing self-help
and self-care subjects. In the summer of 1972, she was
notified by the college that she would be permitted to
matriculate into the college in a regular student status
and to work toward a General Education Diploma.

"I don't have a major," says Julie, "it's called Individual Development."

"She still has crossed wires when it comes to thinking and being able to write it," her mother says, "but she's started typing, and I think maybe that will help."

As for her other interests, outside of school, Julie is comparable to many other teen-agers. "Well, I'm into karate and stuff like that. . . . For some reason, I'm not too involved with people, you know. . . . Chasing after guys, getting jobs, and stuff like that. I mean, normal. I got my driver's license. I've been driving for a year."

Julie is a talkative young women, and, in interviewing her, this author was struck by her understanding of her situation and her ability to express herself. A portion of the interview, edited only in minor form for clarity, follows, in order that the reader might share in the thoughts of Julie West.

> J.H.: We are discovering that something like 2½ per cent of the children in this country have learning disabilities or are retarded, and of this number comparatively few have been identified as having these problems. And, of course, even fewer have the opportunity to be involved in Special Olympics.
>
> JULIE: Of course, I think there's too much about what's normal.
>
> J.H.: I'd hate to have you in one of my classes. This is what my students say all the time, and I—
>
> JULIE: Well, really, normal in the dictionary doesn't really explain it.
>
> J.H.: And there are people all over who never really

look in the dictionary. There are a lot of kids who go to college who don't. I tell them all the time, "You'd better look up the definition of college, because otherwise you're not going to know what you're getting." I don't know how you ever got to be classified—

JULIE: Well, mainly because of my learning difficulties, because I was reading below grade [level].

J.H.: How are you reading now?

JULIE: Oh, it's improving, I'm up to seventh grade. Of course, part of that's due to dyslexia, whatever it is.

J.H.: Dyslexia.

JULIE: Yes, reverse words, and stuff like that. But I look at it this way: you just go around and you learn it different ways, in your brain.

J.H.: That's true, but you certainly are able to understand and articulate what your difficulties are. Do you understand what dyslexia is?

JULIE: Yes, I got it explained to me.

J.H.: In terms of reading, did you know that the average reading level in this country is about—

JULIE: Yes, about sixth grade.

J.H.: And the New York *Times* is written on an eighth-grade level.

JULIE: I read it.

J.H.: If you're reading on a seventh-grade level, you're above average. . . . Well, I don't think you're going to have any problems. I don't even know why I'm interviewing you.

JULIE: (horrible noises) I've listened to psychologists when they're doing their trip, and it's kind of interesting. You'd better get your dictionary out.

J.H.: That's true. It gets to the point where the jargon, the labels, obscure the underlying human potential.

JULIE: Don't you think that's the society, that's just the way we've got it set up?

J.H.: I think it is the society, and one of the things we are trying to do with this book is to get society to look at the exceptional child in a different way, and to encourage parents who have exceptional children to let them out of the closet.

JULIE: I think in the long run it's happening.

J.H.: What do you hope to do now?

JULIE: First, I'm going to get my GED thing [General Education Diploma], you know what that is?

J.H.: Yes.

JULIE: And after that I don't know; I like to take one step at a time.

With respect to the Special Olympics, Julie feels that the program has helped her, like many other youngsters, to gain confidence. And it has given her the opportunity to travel to places to which she otherwise might not have gone. While she still attends area and state meets, rather in the position of a visiting celebrity, Julie no longer participates, even though she could.

"There was a time when I had to kind of sit back and take stock," she says. "I figured that it's time for something else. Seriously, I got too old for it. And I kind of wanted other people to have the same experiences I had."

"I pledge allegiance . . . to the flag . . . of the United States of America. . . ." The slight, dark-haired boy up on the platform spoke gravely, measuring his words, allowing just the right pause between phrases. He stood ramrod straight, his chest puffed out, for to be up on that platform was a great honor. He had been selected to lead the entire assemblage in the Pledge at the 1973 Maryland Special Olympics Games. Few who watched Karl Wiedel as he completed his solemn duty could have suspected that once this little boy was not expected ever to walk normally or to read or even to live to the age of twelve. Yet Karl had disproved all those negative expectations, with the help of a concerned and loving family, a fine school and teachers, and an energetic program of physical activity centered around the Special Olympics—not to mention a lot of courage and effort on his own part.

It was not long after Karl was born that his parents, Mr. and Mrs. Robert Wiedel, realized that something was wrong. "He didn't look the way I would say my other children had looked," Mrs. Wiedel says; "he couldn't hold his milk down, and he screamed, not just cried, but screamed." Mrs. Wiedel told her pediatrician of her worry and on his advice took Karl to a neurosurgeon, who, after examining the little boy, uttered the words the Wiedels feared most to hear. He told them that Karl suffered from brain damage.

How did the Wiedels deal with the news? "You just don't," Mrs. Wiedel says, "not at first. It's like if your kid went out and got crushed or somebody tells you your father dies. Just something goes Boom! and you go numb. The hardest part was the finding out, and the inkling, you know, that something was wrong before we found out.

"I think we went through so much the first three years that we didn't really stop to think about it," Mrs. Wiedel adds. "It was a hard three years."

Karl had a hernia operation at the age of three months. He had two or three spinal taps. His esophagus did not function properly and he had to be fed intravenously. He could not swallow. His muscles did not develop; they were completely flaccid. He was termed a Grecian dwarf, and for the first three years of his life his home was a hospital. His mother and father were people who visited him and brought him toys. The people who cared for him twenty-four hours a day were nurses and doctors.

The Wiedels were hopeful that, once he was released from the hospital, Karl would be able to lead a somewhat normal life. But the neurosurgeon who had first diagnosed Karl's problem cautioned them not to be overoptimistic. It was possible that Karl would never walk, and if he did walk it would not be normally. Also, what with his brain damage and other physical problems, Karl was not expected to live very long. Mrs. Wiedel recalls the doctor's advice: "He said you have to look at it this way: He could live to be ten, or he could die tomorrow. He said take him as he is, treat him like the other children."

When Karl came home from the hospital, this was just what the Wiedels, including Karl's two older brothers, Gary and Skip, tried to do, although, as Mrs. Wiedel says, "It took a lot of explaining to the two older boys, and I think it was hard on them, too, growing up at that time."

For many parents of retarded children, what other people will think or how others will react to seeing the child is a source of worry and embarrassment. They feel that if they take their child out in public, strangers will look at them as if there is something wrong with them. Fortunately for Karl, the Wiedels did not feel this way.

"Wherever we went, he went," says Mrs. Wiedel. ". . . we didn't care if people looked, he was our child not theirs."

Refusing to be embarrassed about Karl was an important step for the Wiedels. But it was a passive step. For a child like Karl to develop to his full potential, his family must also take an active part in encouraging that development, and the Wiedels employed some rather imaginative means particularly to help him develop physically.

Because of an improperly functioning esophagus, Karl could swallow only the softest foods. "I think my banana bill was larger in a year than any other food bill, because that was the thing he could handle the easiest," Mr. Wiedel says. "We kept trying to get him to eat other things, and after a while he started doing so. But all those years of bananas!"

The Wiedels had been warned that Karl might not

walk at all, and he might not have if the family had not taken an active role in encouraging him to walk.

"We used to put heavy concentrations of starch in his clothes," Mrs. Wiedel says. "His muscles were so flaccid. He couldn't even sit up, he had to be propped. But we did exercises with him, to give him muscle tone, and we encouraged him to get from place to place by himself. Naturally, he wanted to be where the other boys were, and they were great. They wouldn't go to him, they'd make him come to them. He'd try and he'd try, and he made it."

"When he stood at three years old, it was unbelievable," says Mr. Wiedel. "It took him about a year to learn how to really walk, much longer than a normal child, but once he did stand he never fell down, and that's something a normal child does do. That first year, Karl wouldn't move unless he could hold on to something, and his arm muscles strengthened because of that. And once he was really walking he was not only walking but running, too."

Once Karl was able to walk, he was rewarded by being allowed to accompany his brothers when they went to play sports. "He spent a lot of time with the boys and their friends," says Mr. Wiedel, "and they didn't mind basically, because he wasn't a nuisance. He knew that even though things weren't how they should have been with him, he couldn't make a nuisance of himself. If he wanted to go he had to behave."

Later, both boys played high school sports, greatly encouraged by Mr. Wiedel. "I was always the type of guy," he says, "who would get up early in the morning when it was about eight degrees out and the wind was blowing, and I'd take the oldest down to play a soccer game and the second oldest over to a football field. They were always playing in some league. And the little one didn't have the same chance, and he wanted it. He'd see the other children his age playing baseball and he'd talk all the time about baseball and growing up and playing the other sports his brothers played."

But the Wiedels did not allow Karl to play baseball with the other kids his age, or any other sports except with his brothers under controlled conditions. Understandably, they were very protective of their son, for Karl had been so very ill as a baby.

Karl did not start school until he was a year older than the usual enrollment age. He was not placed in a special school, but in the kindergarten of a regular school, and he did not look at all out of place. He was very small for his age and in fact looked younger than some of his five-year-old classmates.

The Wiedels know, in retrospect, that it was a mistake to place Karl in a regular school; but they had seen him develop physically beyond the expectations of the doctors who had treated him as a baby, and they hoped that he might be able to make it intellectually in a regular school. But while Karl might not have looked out of place in his kindergarten class, as time went on it became increasingly evident that he did not belong there. As his classmates matured socially and developed the skills they would need in later years of school, Karl's development lagged far behind.

Yet, neither Mr. and Mrs. Wiedel nor the school was

prepared to pronounce Karl unable to cope with the school environment, for to do so would have been to accept the fact of his retardation. Their reluctance was understandable; he had come so far. But when Karl had shown no progress after a second year in kindergarten, his parents were forced to admit that he would be better off in a special school.

The school the Wiedels chose was the Benedictine School for Exceptional Children, located amidst the rolling, green-forested hills of Ridgely, Maryland, and they have never regretted their choice. The school's program is geared to the development of each child to the limits of his potential academically, physically, emotionally, and socially in order that he might become self-supporting. After graduating at age seventeen or eighteen, most of the students go on to habilitation training at the school, and contact is maintained with all graduates for the next ten or twenty years.

When Karl arrived at the Benedictine School he was eight years old, although he looked about six. He also had one of the lowest IQs of any resident at the school, lower than that usually required for admission. Yet the school authorities accepted Karl, after careful study of Karl's history and after talking with him and his parents, for they recognized his potential.

It was quite evident that Karl had been living in a very protective environment. "He wasn't able to tie his shoes when he came," recalls Sister Kevin Toy, teacher, dorm mother, and swimming instructor. "His shirt tail was always out. We had to work with him a lot on self-help skills. He didn't even think about combing his hair."

Academically, Karl was as undeveloped as he was in his self-help skills. "He was unable to read or write or recognize alphabet letters," says Sister Kevin, in whose readiness level class Karl was first placed, "but he was quite a talker."

Karl responded well to the individualized instruction given at the school, and when it was observed that he was keenly interested in sports, material on sports was used to encourage his reading skills. Mr. and Mrs. Wiedel took out a subscription to the Baltimore *Sun* for him so that he could try reading the sports page.

Meanwhile, Karl, like all the other students at the school, was engaged in an active program of athletic training geared toward the Special Olympics, with which the Benedictine School had been associated since the early days of the Special Olympics program. Coach Curt Conley, a regional co-ordinator for Maryland Special Olympics, is physical education teacher at the school.

"I came here in 1972," says Conley, "and the whole focus was on the Special Olympics. You train for the Special Olympics Games, you gear your whole program toward Special Olympics—basketball, floor hockey, track and field, volleyball. What Special Olympics covers could span an entire physical education curriculum. It's a fantastic program, and I just wish more people would become involved with it.

"I taught in a regular high school, and the difference in response between normal and retarded kids is so great. When you see a child go out there and give everything he's got, and even more sometimes, there is nothing else you can ask for."

As soon as Karl arrived at the Benedictine School he was placed in the physical education program, and there he got the opportunity to play sports that his parents had been afraid to allow him. For years he had watched his brothers play baseball and kickball, and he took to such sports immediately. But, he could not swim, and he was very apprehensive about trying.

"It was a very long process teaching Karl to swim," Sister Kevin Toy remembers, "particularly at first—getting him to swim in the shallow end of the pool and to put his face in the water. Even now he swims with his head above the water and his mouth wide open. He breathes poorly because of the disorders of his esophagus and trachea, but, you know, the little kid never gave up.

"I can remember the first day I asked him to try the deep end of the pool. He said, 'Okay, if you'll swim next to me,' and I agreed. I kept telling him, 'Keep going, Karl, keep going,' but I have an idea that he would have done it even if I hadn't prodded him. He tries so hard at everything."

Karl participated in the Special Olympics for the first time in 1971. At that time, he was still learning to swim, so he entered track and field events, among them the 25- and 50-yard dashes. He did well enough in these events to be chosen one of the children from the Benedictine School to participate in the 1971 Maryland Special Olympics Games. Mr. and Mrs. Wiedel had misgivings about Karl's overexerting himself and becoming too excited in the strange surroundings of the state games, but when they were assured that the experience would be good for him they consented to take him.

The entire Wiedel family attended those first State Olympics Games in which Karl participated, and as they observed him with his fellow students from the Benedictine School, talking animatedly between events, marching purposefully with the delegation from the school during the opening ceremonies, they marveled at the poise he had gained in just a few months at the school. But when it came time for Karl to participate in the 50-yard run, Mr. and Mrs. Wiedel suddenly wondered if they had not made a mistake. The hot Maryland sun pounded down on the young racers as they took off along the dusty track that suddenly seemed endless. Toward the head of the group ran a tiny determined figure, legs pumping as fast as they could go, mouth wide open sucking oxygen into the too-small trachea, face beet red from the exertion. Tears streamed down the Wiedels' faces as they watched their little boy, who at one time had not been expected to walk, race down the final stretch. Reaching the 50-yard line at last, Karl nearly collapsed from exhaustion, and suddenly the Wiedels were afraid.

"His mother thought it was too much for him," Sister Kevin recalls, "too much for his heart and all. I said, 'It's not too much for him, Mrs. Wiedel, if he's happy doing it, if he can do it. . . .'"

When Karl, as third-place medal winner, took his position on the platform with the other winners of the event, he was so excited that he could hardly stand still, and there was no question about how he felt about participating in the Special Olympics.

Karl worked hard the following year, training for the Special Olympics Games. His training showed definite results, for in the 1972 State Games, he won third place in the 220-yard run. Progressing from third place in the 50-yard dash to third place in the 220-yard run is a remarkable achievement in stamina alone, not to mention muscular development.

Nineteen seventy-three has to be considered Karl's banner year in the Special Olympics, for it was in this year that he was chosen to lead the entire assemblage in the Pledge of Allegiance, standing up on the speakers platform among all the visiting dignitaries.

"After he did that, he won so many hearts, everybody was just nutsy about him," says Sister Kevin. "He won the Ronald McDonald Medal for Bravery, because he stood up there and said the Pledge."

The Ronald McDonald Medal for Bravery is a watch, and it was presented to Karl by Artie Donovan of the Baltimore Colts, a team that Karl follows closely.

"Karl was just thrilled about that," says Sister Kevin.

In the events that followed, Karl continued his fine performance. Winner of a bronze medal in each of the two preceding state meets, first in the 50-yard dash and then in the 220-yard run, in 1973, he won third place in the 300-yard run. In addition, he won medals for the first time in two swimming events: second place in the 25-yard freestyle and third place in the 50-yard freestyle. All in all, it was quite a list of accomplishments.

"He was so proud," says Sister Kevin. "He brought his medals to school to show his class. And he also showed them the watch that he got from Ronald McDonald."

Against all odds, Karl was progressing farther and farther.

"He never thought about personal grooming when he first came," says Sister Kevin. "Now he's combing his hair and making sure there's a part in it. Before he comes out to supper now, he makes sure that his hair is combed and his hands are washed. You don't have to remind him, he just knows to do it."

"He's very responsible," Coach Curt Conley adds. "Everyone has a certain job they have to do every day in the dormitory. One will clean up the sinks and one will clean up the trash cans and that type of thing. You know you can count on Karl to get his job done, and you don't have to check on him. He goes into the recreation room until school starts and you don't have to worry about him. I'm sure he's going to be a good prospect for occupational training.

"He tries so hard at everything, and he's well liked by both the teachers and the students because of that. In sports there is nothing he won't attempt, nothing he won't work at until he is as good as he can get."

"He's earned the respect of the older boys because of his competitiveness and his consuming interest in sports," said Sister Kevin in 1974. "At this point the big boys in the school, the ones he really looks up to, call him Weedlebug, and they say, 'Come on, Weedlebug, come watch the game with us tonight.'

"Of course, this involves getting permission from the dorm mother of Karl's dorm, the little boys' dorm, so he can go over to the big boys' dorm to watch the game. Many of us would like to see Karl move up to the intermediate age group dorm, although he still panics when too much is asked of him. He tries to act like the bigger kids do, but you can see that he is unsure of himself."

Like all the other students at the Benedictine School, Karl spends every fifth weekend at home as well as summers and major holidays. During his visits at home, his parents enjoy taking him out, even to run simple errands.

"I'll take him for a walk around the neighborhood or to the supermarket when I go, and it's amazing," says Mr. Wiedel. "People come up and talk to him, and I'll say, 'Who was that?' He'll answer, 'Oh, that was so and so; he lives on a certain street in a certain house.' I wondered how he'd gotten to know all these people and then I found out that it had happened when his brothers had a weekly paper route. Karl would walk the route with them and naturally he talked to everybody he saw. He never forgets a face, or a name.

"It's good that he talks to people like that, although I worry sometimes that someone might take advantage of him. Sometimes I also worry about how people will react to what he says.

"When Karl comes home, he likes to go to a certain tavern; he likes their hamburgers. One time we went there and a friend of ours—luckily, he was a friend—was playing one of the slot machines. Karl walked up and started to watch him play. The guy had put a couple of nickels into the machine and played and he didn't win so he walked away. Karl grabbed him by his sleeve and said, 'You finished?' The guy answered, 'That's right.' Then Karl frowned and said, 'You sure don't go for much do you?'"

"He comes home saying things like that all the time," chuckles Mrs. Wiedel. "You look at him and you want to correct him sometimes. But the way he comes out with it, everybody starts laughing and there's no point in trying to tell him he shouldn't say those things."

Karl has made considerable strides academically as well. "He has only been with us about three or four years and already he has advanced two levels," said Sister Kevin in 1974. "He could not even recognize the letters of the alphabet when he first came. Now he can read. Every day he goes up to the teachers' room and picks up his Baltimore *Sun*. And every day, without fail, he reads the sports section. He has learned enough functional words to comprehend the articles, and if he comes across a word he doesn't know in an article that interests him he'll go and find someone else and ask what the word is."

"He knows what he reads," says Mr. Wiedel proudly. "He knows what the Colts did and who scored the touchdowns and who dropped the pass. He isn't just remembering what he heard about the game on radio or saw on television."

"His perception was very poor when he first came, but it has gotten much better," said Sister Kevin. "He is supposed to be borderline severely retarded, just barely trainable, but he functions much higher. The psychologists can't believe that he can read and that he can do the skill sections on an IQ test that are supposed to be beyond his ability. He'll definitely be job training material, we know this. He's making very good progress in reading, so we think he'll even be able to take our driver's ed course, and be able to drive.

"I wouldn't go so far as to say he will one day be able to take his place in society without the help of his father and mother. But it could possibly happen. We have a boy who just graduated, Warren Long. He has won sixteen medals in the Special Olympics Games and holds three state records, two in swimming and one in softball throwing. Winning helped to give him the confidence he needed. Warren can't read or write, but he can drive a car. He memorized all the traffic signs. He can operate any kind of machine and has an outdoor maintenance job in the community. When he is twenty-one he's going to marry a girl he met at the job training center. So, I wouldn't say it would be impossible for Karl to progress in the next five or six years to the point where he could be on his own."

Karl was chosen to participate in the 1974 Maryland Special Olympics Games held at Towson State College in Towson, Maryland, on June 7 and 8. As this was his fourth trip to the State Games, he was definitely a veteran Special Olympian and he behaved accordingly, explaining to less seasoned participants what was taking place on the field, waving to fellow medal winners against whom he had competed in former years.

Fourteen hundred youngsters participated in the 1974 Maryland Special Olympics Games, the largest number in the history of the Maryland program. Karl entered three events, and did better than he had the previous year: third place in the 220-yard run, second place in the 25-yard freestyle, and second place in the 50-yard freestyle.

The Wiedels and their middle son were there for both

days of the games. Their older son, having graduated from college and working in another part of the state, was expected to fly down for the second day. No longer do they worry about Karl's overexerting himself at the games. They realize that the Special Olympics has been good for him, and they support the program whole-heartedly.

Enthusiastic parents, a fine school, and a wonderful program of year-round sports training focused on the Special Olympics have combined to help Karl Wiedel prog-ress far beyond original expectations of his develop-ment.

Practically his whole world is sports, whether partici-pating himself or watching and reading about professional athletes. His favorite football player is Joe Namath; bas-ketball player, Elvin Hayes; baseball players, Fred Cog-gins and Mel Bumery, because they are both outfielders who run a lot. He will try any type of sport activity. In fact, he is eager to learn to ski.

The Special Olympics has enabled Karl to feel that he is participating in sport activity in a similar manner to other children. As Mr. Wiedel says, "Karl would see the other children his age playing sports and competing, and he never had a shot at anything before the Special Olympics. Now he's been given something by this pro-gram that society really can't give him—a chance to par-ticipate and to win."

Mrs. Wiedel adds, "It makes him feel like his older brothers when he can say, 'I'm going to be in track today, and I've got swimming.' And now he says, 'This is my weekend.' And no one is supposed to take over the spotlight. He knows it's his time to shine."

Karl now has thirteen medals, which he proudly displays on his wall. He also has a number of photographs, of which he is equally proud, showing his participation in various regional and state meets. In conversation with this author, Karl expressed interest in the photographs that had been taken of him at the 1974 Maryland Special Olympics:

J.H.: "Would you like some of the pictures?"

KARL: "Yes."

J.H.: "All right, I'll send you some."

KARL: "The ones I got yesterday! The ones I got yesterday!"

J.H.: "When you were swimming? You want them more than the running pictures?"

KARL: "I want them, too."

Karl has received the pictures he requested, and no doubt they have been placed with the other things—the trophies and medals—that show that he, too, can play sports and compete and win, just like other kids. The Special Olympics program has, in large measure, made this possible.

"You know," says Mr. Wiedel, "Karl can't be insured. I inquired about it a year ago, and the man said, 'I'm sorry, there's no way—his heart.' I told him what Karl did and he said, 'You mean he swims 50 yards and runs the 220? Did you ever take him to a doctor?' I said we had. He said, 'What did the doctor say?' I answered, 'Let him live every day to the fullest.'

"That's exactly what's going to happen," says Mr. Wiedel. "You don't want to think about the dangers, but what are you going to do, keep him in a cage? This is what he wants to do, and if he makes it he makes it, and if he doesn't, that's the name of the game."

Few children, "normal" or not, exhibit such a desire to live, such a zest for life. Perhaps Coach Curt Conley expressed best what all the good things that have happened to this small boy mean to Karl:

"He's always a child who wakes up in the morning and —Well, you just know it's going to be a good day for him, you know?"

AFTERWORD

The young people presented in the previous pages are not "typical" Special Olympians. In fact, there is no such thing as a "typical" Special Olympian. The people who participate in the program range from those like little Stevie Waddell, who had to be helped from the swimming pool after his event but whose face beamed with joy at having finished, to the fifty-three- and fifty-nine-year-old participants in the Indiana Special Olympics, to some like Susan Conn's boyfriend, Rick, who said he didn't like the Special Olympics Games but might try again, to someone like Julie West.

They are of different ages, sexes, races; they come from different areas of the country, from different backgrounds; they cover the range of levels of retardation. What they have in common is that they have had the opportunity to *participate*, to *compete* as other people do in a program of physical activity that stresses doing one's best more than winning or losing. Different participants have derived different things from the Special Olympics. For some it has been increased muscular co-ordination and ability to concentrate; for others, improved physical appearance; for still others, an opportunity to get away from a confining environment, to travel and to meet new people. For all, there has been the opportunity to feel what Special Olympics calls "a new kind of joy."

It is hoped that this book will encourage greater participation in the Special Olympics, that previously uninvolved citizens will initiate Special Olympics programs in their areas or become involved in already existing programs, that parents and teachers of retarded children who do not participate will see that these children have the opportunity to do so, and that states and localities will realize the importance of regular, year-round physical education for their special children and make the necessary commitment to such programs.

The retarded need not be excluded from the rest of society. The Special Olympics has proven this. But we have shut them out for so long, it is up to us to welcome them back in.

APPENDIX—SPECIAL OLYMPICS MILESTONES

1963   Kennedy Foundation and American Association for Health, Physical Education and Recreation co-operate on a physical fitness program for the mentally retarded and offer awards for achievement.

1968, July   First International Special Olympics Games in Chicago.

1968, August   Senator Edward Kennedy announces the establishment of Special Olympics, Inc., with Eunice Kennedy Shriver as president.

1968, November First annual meeting of the Board of Directors of Special Olympics, Inc., Los Angeles.

1969, Summer   Eight regional games, 18 state-wide games and an estimated 400 local games are held, involving some 68,000 children.

1970, January   All fifty states, the District of Columbia and Canada have Special Olympics organizations and State Directors.

1970, March   The National Hockey League Board of Governors announces sponsorship of an International Special Olympics Floor Hockey Program.

1970, March   550 young athletes participate in the first French Special Olympics Games—the first instance of significant participation outside the United States.

1970, August   150,000 Special Olympians and 65,000 vol-
                    unteers now involved in more than 1,400
                    local and area meets.

1970, August   Second International Special Olympics
                    Games take place in Chicago with 2,000
                    athletes from fifty states, the District of Co-
                    lumbia, Canada, France, and Puerto Rico.

1971, December   U. S. Olympic Committee gives Special
                    Olympics officials approval as one of only
                    two organizations entitled to use the name
                    "Olympics."

1972, June   Jean Claude Killy, world champion skier,
                    welcomes 1,500 French athletes to French
                    Special Olympics Games.

1972, August   Third International Games are held on the
                    campus of the University of California at
                    Los Angeles with 2,500 participants.

1973, April   ABC TV broadcasts segment covering Spe-
                    cial Olympics on "Wide World of Sports."

1973, June   Pierre Mazeaud, French Minister of Youth
                    and Sports, attends French Special Olym-
                    pics Games. Impressed by the spirit and
                    courage of the athletes, he offers on the
                    spot six silver cups as trophies.

1974, January   More than 300,000 children now active in
                    Special Olympics, year round, including
                    15,000 local training programs, meets, and
                    games.

1974, July   400,000 athletes take part in 1974 Special
                    Olympics program.

1974, December   National Basketball Association and Amer-
                    ican Basketball Association co-operate to
                    sponsor the National Special Olympics
                    Basketball Program.

1975, Spring	3,182 noncommissioned officers run from Washington, D.C., and Los Angeles, California, non-stop in a 3,182-mile marathon for Special Olympics. Hundreds of high school, college track and cross-country teams, jogging associations, and concerned volunteers join to help raise funds to send athletes to the International Special Olympics Games.
1975, April	Mexican athletes compete for the first time in a Special Olympics event held in Nogales, Arizona. Mexico plans to send a delegation to the 1975 International games.
1975, August	Fourth International Special Olympics Games take place with 3,200 young athletes participating from all fifty states, the District of Columbia, and eight foreign countries.
1976, January	More than 500,000 athletes are now involved in the Special Olympics. Eleven foreign countries are sponsoring major Special Olympics programs.